Published by
The Lutterworth Press
P.O. Box 60
Cambridge
CB1 2NT
England

e-mail: publishing@lutterworth.com
website: http://www.lutterworth.com

ISBN 0 7188 9093 0 paperback

British Library Cataloguing in Publication Data:
A catalogue record is available from the British Library.

First published 1962
Reprinted 2002

CONTENTS

FOREWORD

As a part of their current study on "The Word of God and the Church's Missionary Obedience", the Working Committee of the Department of Missionary Studies jointly run by the International Missionary Council and the World Council of Churches decided to commission a survey and appraisal of recent work in Biblical theology having any bearing upon the nature and necessity of the Church's mission to the world. Dr. J. Blauw, of the Netherlands Missionary Council, kindly accepted their invitation to undertake this task. At the same time a series of consultations was planned in America, Asia, Europe, and Africa, to be attended chiefly by people responsibly engaged in the Churches' missionary work, at which this and other material was to form the basis for discussion. These conferences were to be followed up by the writing, and careful theological scrutiny, of a book by Dr. D. T. Niles[1] dealing with the empirical issues which arise today in connection with Christian missions. This whole study, focused in the publication of these two books, seeks to answer the question "What does it mean in theological terms and in practice in this ecumenical era for the Church to discharge its mission to all the nations?"

We are very grateful to Dr. Blauw for admirably fulfilling his assignment, and to the Netherlands Missionary Council for enabling him to take time for work on this

[1] D. T. Niles, *Upon the Earth: the Mission of God and the Missionary Enterprise of the Churches.*

7

study. We have pleasure in commending this constructive presentation of a critical survey of Biblical theology in this field, believing it to be a real contribution to ecumenical thinking—which concerns itself equally with the mission and the unity of the Church.

VICTOR E. W. HAYWARD
C.W.M.E. Research Secretary

London

INTRODUCTION

DURING the Ghana Assembly of the International Missionary Council, the late Professor W. Freytag made a comparison between 1928 and 1958. In a way so characteristic of him he expressed the difference thus: "Then missions had problems, but they were not a problem themselves."[1]

The problematic character of the missionary movement which began about two and a half centuries ago has led to an ever more insistent question as to the *why* of missions. Not only the method but even the right of missions to exist at all is at stake. For those who see the missionary movement of the last few centuries merely as a historically distinct phenomenon, it is not difficult to consign missions themselves to the great institutions which have had their day, like any other specific historical complex, since missions will of course gradually disappear of their own accord. For what is old and obsolete is at the point of disappearing.

However, when missions are considered not as an historical phenomenon but as a commission from God, the question of a Biblical and theological foundation for mission becomes important.

There was a time when this Biblical foundation and motivation was not considered to be so urgently necessary as is now the case. In fact, the Biblical motive for missions was only one among many motives, and sometimes not even the most important one. The impulses that led to the awakening of missionary work have been varied and multiple in the course of history, and the deposit of all

9

these is plain to see in the history of missionary theory and knowledge.[2]

During the last thirty years, however, a growing resistance has been noted to a multiple foundation for missions, especially on the European continent. The plea has been made with ever greater emphasis for a "purification of the motive for missions" and for an exclusive limitation to a Biblical foundation.[3]

Though this Biblical foundation might not have been lacking in the past, we must admit that the theological basis was often quite narrow, and frequently took little or no account of the important trends in academic theological research.

So far as theology is concerned, missions have often been regarded as a by-product. And when attempts have been made to treat them as a theological problem, the reaction from the theological and church side has not been satisfactory. At this point a great change has come about in the last few decades. The result of the theology of the Old and New Testament points more and more in the direction of the universal *and* missionary character of the Church; and systematic theology is keeping up its end.[4]

At the same time, there is a felt need in missionary circles for a broader and deeper theological orientation. Not only church and mission, but also theology and missionary thinking, are approaching each other more and more.

The influence of these factors is not always apparent at missionary conferences, perhaps because the themes of such conferences are more often concerned with practical missionary affairs and with missionary leadership rather than with theological sensitivity. Above all, there is always the language barrier, so that the results of theological research in one language area become known only slowly in another language area. In order to fill this existing lacuna to some degree, the attempt is ventured in the following survey to set forth the *most important* results of the theological research of the last thirty years concerning the basis and the purpose, the place and the meaning of missions.

In discussions on missionary work and its distinctive place in the Church, it has been generally agreed that the Church has a missionary calling. The question has been, what is the relation between this calling, the existence of which is not disputed, and the shape it is to take, which *is* a point of dispute in our time and age, and which is usually expressed by the word "missions" (foreign missions, *äussere Mission*).

I had been asked to have this manuscript ready by April 1960. As I was unable to start work upon it till November 1959 and, once I had started, was occupied with other work time and again, it bears clear signs of the haste in which it had to be written. After it had been extensively discussed in Geneva from July 10 to 14, 1960, it appeared to be necessary to add a few things to it. Again this revision had to be postponed till the end of November 1960. This manuscript is now presented to the reader with apologies for not having been able to give anything better.

I would like the reader to take into account the following factors when judging it:

(*a*) This little book is not intended to present a new Biblical theology of missionary work but a *critical survey* of what has been said about the subject by others in the past thirty years. The gaps that will be encountered are therefore indications both of gaps in the theological material and of faulty compilation.

(*b*) I realize that in arranging the large amount of material in such a way that it could be given in the present paper, I have made the treatise more *schematic* than the Biblical data and their theological reflections warrant. Actually the data to be found in the Bible are more varied in character than could be shown in the limited space available. It may be, however, that this gives the book greater practical value.

(c) In view of the amount of material and the task I was given, I restricted myself to the questions that concern what is called the Biblical foundation of missionary work. The important and nowadays burning question of the relation between "the word of God and the living faiths of men" had to remain unanswered or practically so.

(d) I have been asked what is meant by "Biblical theology of missionary work". Personally I take it to mean a conception of missionary work that is as closely as possible related to what the Bible tells us. Every age needs a fresh encounter with the Bible, because every age has its own questions and problems. Nothing is more healthful than to listen to the Bible time and again, *not* because we want to hear the answer to *our* question from the Bible (theological ventriloquy through the medium of the Bible is a favourite but rather tiring and useless pastime), but because we want to miss nothing of the light that God's Word sheds on our path.

Some people will consider my approach to the Holy Bible too conservative, others may consider it too liberal. Some people will think I have let myself be influenced too much by the present-day problems of missionary work, others that I have dealt with the material in too abstract and timeless a way. I admit that as far as the task entrusted to me is concerned, namely, to write a treatise about theological data (exegetic and systematic), I have overstepped the boundaries several times, particularly in the last two chapters and in the notes.

(e) I have also been asked why I have taken the Old Testament as my starting point. Some were of the opinion that this wronged Jesus Christ as God's main revelation. I hasten to declare that I, too, consider the Scriptures precious because they testify of Jesus Christ (John 5: 39), and are realized in Him. The Scriptures have an open horizon turned towards Jesus Christ, but that also means that Jesus Christ has a previous history worth investigating. It is He who gives the Old Testament its perspective and He cannot be understood except in the light of God's actions in history, the history of salvation. That is why this book has been arranged in such a way as to deal with God's actions in history since the creation of the world. It seemed to me illegitimate, theologically speaking, (i) to project Jesus Christ back into the Old Testament and thus to interpret Him into its text; (ii) to surrender to those who exegesize away the Messianic nature of (parts of) the Old Testament.

(f) Finally the author is surrounded by European continental theologians, which means that he has a certain opinion about theological subjects and that he deals with them in a characteristic manner. The author has not been either able or willing to turn himself into a cosmopolitan *in theologicis*. The literature he used was also for the major part of European (continental) origin. There is no doubt that more British and American theological literature now exists in the university libraries than was the case twenty years ago, but there were all too many books that could not be secured and there was not enough time for travelling. So the author wishes to apologize in advance if he has missed out any important works to be found in Great Britain and America. The harvest of missionary ideas from systematic theology has been extremely poor, partly because systematic theology has shown very little interest in the questions with which we deal in this book, partly because the author has been very inaccurate

13

in his research in this respect; exegetic literature claimed practically all his time and attention.

As it has so often been necessary in this survey to refer to others, the author has been in danger of misunderstanding them and/or of reporting their opinions incorrectly. He sincerely hopes that he has succeeded in doing injustice to nobody and that he is capable of listening carefully enough to be able to pass on to others what he has heard.

I am indebted to the International Missionary Council for the honour of this assignment; to the Netherlands Missionary Council for permission to spend time on its fulfilment; especially to Dr. W. L. Holladay, who under pressure of time translated the first draft from the Dutch language; to Dr. A. M. Chirgwin, who reshaped the final text; to the Rev. Drs. J. Slomp, who took care of the notes, bringing them up to the Anglo-Saxon standard; and finally to all those who have helped me through discussing the first draft, in criticizing and stimulating my thoughts.

With the gratitude of a son and the pride of a father, I mention that the indexes of Bible references and of authors have been prepared by my eighty-years old father and my twenty-years old son. This symbolizes the fact that the present generation is nothing without the former, and helpless without the future, generation.

J. BLAUW

June 1961

THE POINT OF DEPARTURE AND GENERAL PERSPECTIVE OF UNIVERSALISM IN THE OLD TESTAMENT

1. Introduction

WHEN THE QUESTION OF THE BASIS AND MEANING of the mission of the Church to all the nations is raised, the Old Testament can neither be by-passed nor referred to merely by way of introduction.

There was a time when one scarcely knew what to do with the Old Testament. The search for the motive for mission in the Old Testament was confined to the indication of some non-Israelite persons who were incorporated into Israel or who accepted the faith of Israel (Ruth and Naaman, for example), and to the unearthing from prophetic writings of testimonies to universalism which also bear a missionary character to a greater or lesser degree. The most popular subjects were Jonah and the so-called Deutero-Isaiah. Thus in this respect the older literature is constantly disappointing.[1]

This should not come as too much of a surprise to us. For years Old Testament criticism was, with few exceptions, more impressed by the *dependence* of the Old Testament on its environment than by its special *vocation in the midst* of this environment. Historical and literary criticism had little interest in a "theology of the Old Testament" in the sense attached to this expression at the present time.

In the last thirty years a great change has taken place. So far as I know, W. Eichrodt was the first to take a new direction, in his *Theologie des Alten Testaments*, which appeared in 1933–35 (E.T. *Theology of the Old Testament*).

15

Since then several theologies of the Old Testament have appeared which go further in the direction taken by Eichrodt.[2] The most recent publication in this area is that of G. von Rad: *Theologie des Alten Testaments, Band I: Die Theologie der geschichtlichen Uberlieferungen,* Ch. Kaiser Verlag, Munich, 1957–60 (E.T. in preparation, *Theology of the Old Testament,* Vol. I: *The Theology of the Historical Traditions*). In more than one respect this work is especially instructive for our purpose, because von Rad is particularly concerned to understand the kerygma of the Old Testament.[3] To this end he does not draw up a dogmatic scheme, thereupon to go looking in the Old Testament for answers to the questions asked of him; instead he attempts to understand the Old Testament in the context in which it has come to us. He leaves the material in the context of *Heilsgeschichte* (salvation-history), in which it has been placed by Israel herself. He considers *recital* to be the most legitimate form of theological discussion about the Old Testament.[4]

Now it is striking that since more attention has come to be paid to the whole peculiar character of Israel and its "religion" in the midst of the nations, the *message* of Israel and the *place* of Israel stand out much more clearly.

Therefore we are also in a happier position than we were thirty years ago, as regards the Old Testament foundation of mission. Where *Heilsgeschichte* stands out again in its own right, mission comes into the picture too. The *heilsgeschichtlich* (salvation-historical) foundation of mission has a long history, and it would seem that a new chapter to this history can now be added,[5] which in essence is nothing but an elaboration of one of the first chapters. The clearer becomes the view of the unity of the Bible, the greater appears the value of visions which, while they date from a "pre-critical" age, nevertheless appear more correct than we used to think.[6]

We consider it of great importance that a "theology of mission" be based not only on the narrow strip of some "missionary texts", but on the whole witness of both the Old Testament and the New Testament. That this is the case in regard to the Old Testament must now be demonstrated in this chapter.

Perhaps it would not be superfluous to call attention to the not unimportant distinction between "universal" and "missionary".

When we call the message of the Old Testament "universal", we mean that it has the whole world in view and that it has validity for the whole world. This universality is the *basis* for the missionary message of the Old Testament. By "missionary" we understand the commission to deliberate witness, to going out. Our thesis, which will be set forth below, is that we must be much more reserved in speaking of the missionary message of the Old Testament than of its universal message.

2. *Point of Departure*

As our point of departure we choose the first chapters of the Bible, Gen. 1–11. This is not so self-evident as it seems. Ordinarily the exodus from Egypt forms the point of departure both in the theologies of the Old Testament and in the description of the history of Israel.

But it is no coincidence that the Old Testament has been handed down to us in its present form. The *arrangement, the order of the material* also belongs to the kerygma, the message of the Old Testament. Historical and literary criticism have proved that there are various sources and strata in the Old Testament tradition; but we need not concern ourselves with this at the present juncture. Our problem is the kerygma, and this kerygma can be neither preserved nor passed on properly if some point of departure is chosen other than that given by the Old Testament itself in its traditional form. Therefore for an understanding of the universal purport of the Old Testament, it is necessary to have the Old Testament begin where it begins. As long ago as 1936, K. Hartenstein pointed out (albeit in another connection) that the first chapters of Genesis are of special significance for a theology of mission.[7] But he left this remark without elaboration, and it is now time for us to follow up this hint of his. This can all the more easily be done, now that exegetical research is providing us with increasing light.[8]

The first chapters of Genesis are (as is the whole Book of Genesis, for that matter) a key to the understanding of all the rest of the Old Testament and even, for those who recognize the unity of the Bible, of the whole Bible.

The conviction that we are to look upon these beginning chapters not only as an adaptation of very old narrative material, but more especially as a "theology of history", and as *rückwarts gekehrte Prophetie* (prophecy turned backwards) is gaining ground more and more.[9] We shall therefore have to put aside the thought that we are being offered here an "ontology" of creation and of man. We shall have to dispense with this philosophical terminology and mode of thinking, in order not to lose sight of the true intentions of these very compact and charged chapters. Israel did not think and live philosophically, but historically, and the Old Testament, more than any other document from these times, has a historical, prophetic character. As history, the Old Testament is prophecy; as prophecy, it is at the same time history.

The first chapters of Genesis must therefore be seen also as witness, as confession concerning the *pre*-history of Israel as the People of God, and at the same time as *pre*-history which gives meaning to the history of Israel itself.

In short compass the contents of this "pre-history" may be summed up as follows.

In the beginning God created the heavens and the earth. The whole creation has been instituted *upon* man and for man (Gen. 1). In consequence the centre of creation is man (Gen. 2), but man misuses this centrality and does not understand his responsibility (Gen. 3). Then there begins the guilty alienation from God which assumes

18

ever more catastrophic proportions, and which makes itself felt in the whole creation (Gen. 4–6). Judgment, then, cannot fail to come (Gen. 7–8), but after this judgment, and through it, God still remains faithful to His creation and to man (Gen. 8, 9). A new generation of men grows up (Gen. 10), but these also turn away from God and presumptuously seek only themselves and look only to themselves. Again the judgment of God strikes man, this time not in a Flood but in the dispersion of mankind over the whole earth as a result of their alienation from each other (Gen. 11).

Here we have a conception both of the origin and of the history of the earth and the world of nations which is of an uncommon "theological" quality.[10]

Now this relationship of God to the world of nations is the background of the history of Israel, which begins with the patriarchs and particularly with the call of Abraham.[11]

The call of Abraham, and the history of Israel which begins at that point, is the beginning of the restoration of the lost unity of mankind and of the broken fellowship with God. "In you all the families of the earth will be blessed" (or "will bless themselves"), Gen. 12: 3[12] Here it becomes clear *that the whole history of Israel is nothing but the continuation of God's dealings with the nations, and that therefore the history of Israel is only to be understood from the unsolved problem of the relation of God to the nations.*

[This connection of what has been called *Urgeschichte*, primeval history (Gen. 1–11) and the history of the origin of Israel (Gen. 12 ff.) has been convincingly indicated by von Rad.[13] A complete exegesis of chapters 10–12: 9 of Genesis lies outside the scope of this book, but the main lines may be set forth here. In the Table of the Nations in Gen. 10 we have a consequence of the announcement in Gen. 9 regarding the new covenant with the earth. This covenant shows its effectiveness in the filling of the earth with a multitude of the nations. The joy of the Creator has won out over his sadness and wrath (cf. Acts 17: 26). The world of nations is the result of the peace made with man *after* the Flood.

The nations are simultaneously signs of God's will to peace and of His judgment. It is from this double point of view that the nations will be considered, again and again, in the whole Old Testament. The key to understanding this ambivalent assessment is put into our hands in Gen. 10 and 11. They contain the reflection of Israel on the problem of the nations (or the heathen) and the fundamental kerygma regarding the nations.

Nevertheless, the story of the Tower of Babel does not carry the same weight as does that of the List of Nations, because the confusion of language and the dispersion over the whole earth are counterbalanced by the call of Abraham and the election of Israel. Even in the choice of words Gen. 12: 1–3 recalls the story of the Tower of Babel. The promise to Abraham reflects both the salvation of God (Gen. 10) and the judgment of God (Gen. 11), but salvation prevails (cf. "him who curses you", singular, with "those who bless you", plural). "Salvation and judgment are now brought into history by God, and by the attitude taken toward this work that God will perform in history, men shall determine the decision made for judgment or salvation." (Von Rad, *1 Mose*, p. 133; E.T., *Genesis*.)

It is possible to see an analogy between the central and decisive part allotted to Abraham in Gen. 12: 3 and the story in Gen. 2: 16 and 17. In the one, Man's answer (Adam=Man=humanity) to God's commandment concerning the tree of knowledge of good and evil decided his life and future, in the other it becomes clear that from then on one's attitude with regard to Abraham will have the same decisive meaning. This implies that God's actions in history in fulfilling His promise to Abraham (that is, to the people of Israel) perform a critical function in the lives of all peoples. In other words, obedience and disobedience towards God are judged against the background of those people's attitude towards Israel. There is an interaction

20

(which cannot be fully proved exegetically, but which can be derived theologically and anthropologically) between Gen. 1–12 and the remainder of the Old Testament; the history of Israel is the elaboration of what has been related in Gen. 1–11; Gen. 1–11 in its turn is a reflection of Israel's history. Any anthropology based on the Bible will therefore have to take seriously both the portrait of Man as painted in Gen. 1–11 and Israel's reaction to God's action.

An obvious illustration of the data in Gen. 10–12 is Ps. 87.

Here the greatness of Jerusalem, the city of God, is celebrated. This greatness she derives from the fact that she is the city of God. But as the city of God she is at the same time the native city of all nations. They come not only *to* this city, but they have their domicile, their citizenship, their birthright there. As *pars pro toto* we find Egypt (Rahab) and Babylon, Philistia, Tyre, and Ethiopia named. In the history of Israel most of these nations appear as constant arch-enemies of Israel and Israel's God. In an imposing statement from God's own mouth (verse 4), it is declared that they are all at home in the city of God. In an unequivocal way the law of God is declared to be binding on the nations. They have their *origin and destiny* in the same love wherewith Yahweh loves Jerusalem and Israel. This universal love is answered in the glad round-dance of the nations within the city of God: an ecumenical vision which was granted to Israel in worship, as a reminder of the universal lordship and goodness of Israel's God. This song must have been of great significance, particularly for the strangers incorporated into Israel.]

3. Election

If Gen. 1–11 forms the background of the history of the patriarchs, the latter in its turn forms the background of the history of Israel which begins in Exodus.

That the call of Abraham (and thus implicitly that of Israel) must be seen in the light of God's revelation to the nations, is especially to be gleaned from Gen. 12: 3.

[Paul names Abraham in Rom. 4: 13 the heir of the world, and the meeting with Melchizedek, Gen. 14: 18–24, is connected in Heb. 7 with the universal priesthood of Christ. The important declaration of Gen. 12: 3 is interpreted in the New Testament as a promise of salvation for all peoples, and placed in a Christological light (Gal. 3: 8, 16, 29).]

The great importance of this declaration is being admitted more and more. Abraham and his descendants will draw the attention of the nations to themselves and make them eager to share in his blessings. *The act of election of Abraham (and implicitly of Israel) coincides with the promise or prospect of blessing for the nations.*[14] H. H. Rowley (among others) has pointed out in detail this universal meaning of the election of Israel.[15] One might differ with him in opinion as to the *motive* for Israel's election: he supposes that God chose Israel *because* Israel was most fit for the task.[16]

It seems to me that there is no specific basis present in the Old Testament itself for this declaration. In fact, the opposite is often set forth: Deut. 7: 6–8, Amos 9: 7.[17] Emphatically and rightly, however, Rowley maintains that election is "election for service". "The purpose of the election is service, and when the service is withheld the election loses its meaning, and therefore fails."[18] This does not mean, however, that God on His part abandons the election; on the contrary. Special emphasis on this election for *service* is made by Th. C. Vriezen in his basic study on the election of Israel according to the Old Testament; *Die Erwahlung Israels nach dem Alten Testament.*[19]

> The Old Testament is not concerned in the first instance to lay the foundations of a certainty of salvation, and least of all a personal certainty of salvation, but to place the fact of [Israel's] existence as the people of God in the right light:

22

this privilege has not been extended to Israel that she might become infatuated by it, but that she might recognize it as a commission. Election sets Israel apart from the nations, so that she might in a special way serve God and reveal his glory and lordship on earth and in the end bring the whole world to God[20]. . . Election has no goal in itself, but only the Kingdom of God.[21]

It seems to me of the highest importance to take careful note of the specific meaning and import of the word *election*. As Vriezen and Rowley both demonstrate convincingly, it has no connection with favouritism, and there is therefore no ground for the reproach still often heard within the younger Churches of Asia (an echo of the reproach from the neo-Hindu side?): "We do not like a God who has favourite peoples and favourite persons."

As a matter of fact, the idea that the divine deed of election is to be explained as favouritism belongs to the great sin, the apostasy of Israel.[22] It is therefore of great significance that the word *election* and *choice* in the Old Testament, whenever it refers to Israel, is always used in the active, never in the passive form: Israel is never called *bāhūr*, "chosen".[23]

Israel is not so much the *object* of divine election as *subject* in the service asked for by God on the ground of election. Perhaps one could put it this way: that there is not service *through* election but rather election *because of* service. Therefore election is not primarily a privilege but a responsibility. If the responsibility is refused, election can even become the motive for divine punishment: "You only have I known of all the families of the earth, *therefore* I will punish you for all your iniquities" (Amos 3: 2). It is therefore a misjudgment of the clear declarations of the Old Testament to derive from the election of the nation Israel any national concept, much less any sanction for a "master race" or nationalism.[24] The Old Testament is not at all concerned with purity of descent, unity of territory or culture, or the like. The emphasis in the Old Testament never lies upon Israel as a people, but only upon Israel as the People of *God*.[25]

The election of Israel is a matter of divine initiative which has as its goal the recognition of God by all nations over the whole world. The way to this goal is the theocracy of Israel; the means is Israel's separation from the other peoples.[26]

While the emphasis is laid during the whole history of Israel on her necessity to be separate, this must never be explained as an expression of Old Testament "particularism", but as the adherence to the *conditio sine qua non* for the maintenance of theocracy in Israel as the forerunner for the lordship of God over the whole world.

[The exegesis which R. B. Y. Scott has given of Exod. 19: 6, is especially enlightening at this point.[27] In the previous verse (verse 5) the right of possession of all peoples by Yahweh is underlined: ". . . you shall be my own possession among all peoples; for all the earth is mine." Verse 6 says: "And you shall be to me a kingdom of priests and a holy nation." This does not mean that Israel shall be a people that is made up entirely of priests, but that Israel shall fulfil a priestly role as a people in the midst of the peoples; she represents God in the world of nations. What priests are for a people, Israel as a people is for the world.

No doubt the Old Testament is "particularistic", in the sense that salvation and the service of God are confined to one special people; but this "particularism" is the instrument for the universal ends of God with the world. Therefore the word *particularism* is unsuited to define the task and place of Israel. It arouses misunderstandings and associations with isolationism, separatism, individualism. To my way of thinking we will do best to discard the scheme of particularism and universalism in the light of the theology of the Old Testament in our days.[28]

Alongside of declarations such as Exod. 19: 6, we might further cite such Psalms as 67, 96, 100, 117, etc. The oft-used term "holy" as a designation for Israel also points in this direction. By "holy" (*qādhòš*) is meant not an ethical quality but a relation with God; consecrated (and thus also separated) for a special service.[29]]

4. The Nations

If the election of Abraham, i.e. Israel, is to have a universal purpose, the consequence of it for the world of nations is that they can be described as "peoples whom Yahweh does not know". The designation "nations" is identical with "heathen"; in other words, the designation "nations" (*goyyim*) does not have a political or national, but a religious meaning.[30]

It is not possible here to treat in broad outline the place and meaning of the nations in the Old Testament. But it is worth while here to assemble the results of research in a few statements.

(i) The Old Testament does not state that the election of Israel means the rejection of the nations. The fact that the Old Testament knows nothing of the passive definition (that Israel is the chosen people), but the active announcement that Yahweh chooses, makes it impossible to speak of the nations as "rejected". And this never occurs in the Old Testament.

(ii) The nations come into view variously in the Old Testament, but always *in their relation to Israel* as the people of God. It is out of the question, then, to speak of a uniform judgment on the nations; on the contrary, it is always a question of their *concrete relation* to Israel. In other words, the distinction between Israel and the nations is exclusively connected with God's dealings.[31] In principle, then, the possibility is always open for reception into Israel as the people of God and for *sharing* in the salvation and blessing of Israel.

(iii) Often, particularly in the historical books of the Old Testament, the nations are a *threat* to Israel in politics and a *temptation* in respect to religion. Whenever Israel

25

cannot withstand the temptation to consort with the gods of the nations, and whenever it has let itself be yoked with them, it has lost its sense and right of existence, and has been threatened and conquered by them. This is the way the judgment of Yahweh works: He punishes Israel for her infidelity and uses the nations as His instrument.

(iv) The nations are *witnesses* of Yahweh's deeds in Israel. This is their most prominent function. In God's dealings with Israel, however, they, too, are summoned to recognize the God of Israel as the God of the whole earth. The existence of other gods was never theoretically denied; in the light of Yahweh's deeds, however, they are unimportant and powerless. That God's dealings with Israel *directly* concern the nations comes explicitly and clearly to light in the Psalms (e.g. 22: 28, 24: 1, 33: 8, 47: 8, 48: 10, 66: 7, 67, 87, 93-100, 117, etc. etc.).

[The opening of a psalm of the nations, Psalm 67, is quite plain in this regard; Israel prays: "May God be gracious to us [Israel] and bless us, and make his face to shine upon us, *that* thy way may be known upon earth, thy saving power among all nations" (verses 1-2). The conclusion is still shorter and more pregnant (verse 7): "God has blessed us; let all the ends of the earth fear him!"* The same thought is found in Ps. 117 and elsewhere.]

The nations are also created (Ps. 86: 9) and summoned by their relation to Israel to praise (i.e. to recognize) the God of the whole earth (Exod. 19: 5, Deut. 32: 8, Psalms *passim*).

(v) The recognition by the nations of Yahweh, the God of Israel, as the God of the earth is anticipated by the message of the prophets, who involve the nations most intensively in their preaching. In this regard there is complete unanimity in all the prophets.[32] The question in Israel *and* in the world of nations is not the existence,

* The Dutch version reads ". . . *that* all the ends of the earth may fear him", and Dr. Blauw has underlined "*that*".

but the presence of God.[33] The active presence of God is *the* problem of world history.[34]

It is no coincidence that in the prophetic books of the Old Testament the nations come to the fore so frequently in a different perspective from that in the historical books.[35] It is in the light of the exile that the special task and place of Israel in the world of nations becomes plain. In every case the downfall of Israel means not the downfall of the "national" god, as is considered self-evident among all the nations, because Israel's God is not a local divinity, but the Creator of heaven and earth. The promised restoration of Israel, according to Ezekiel, has the same motive as had the downfall of Israel: and you (Israel, the nations) shall know that I am Yahweh. The prevalent judgment on the nations in the Old Testament finds here its basis and unity.

(vi) The recognition of Yahweh by the nations is usually set forth as *imperative* and the *future* as *summons* and as *promise*. This summons is the meaning of Israel's history and the contents of her liturgy. During the whole history of Israel this comes to realization little if at all.[36] It is ordinarily expressed in this way so that the universal character of the Old Testament, of Israel's history, is eschatologically defined.[37] This eschatology is brought to bear especially on the return of Israel from exile, as the immediate goal. But this return will be an evidence that Israel's God is indeed the only living God, an evidence that *must* convince the nations.

(vii) This eschatological outlook is often connected with the expectation of the Messiah.[38] At the point where this universal expectation of salvation comes out in the prophets, there is a living reminder of God's power and right as *Creator* (notably in the so-called Deutero-Isaiah).

5. *Summary and Conclusions*

If we may summarize what we have said thus far regarding the universal point of departure and purport for universalism in the Old Testament in general, we cannot do better than quote the words of one of the few systematic theologians who have given attention to the problem that confronts us, Karl Barth:

> The history of Israel in her totality and in her context is universal prophecy. For the Old Testament makes it unmistakably clear, again and again, that it is precisely the covenant of Yahweh with a unique Israel, of Israel with a unique God . . . far from being an end in itself, far from getting one wrapped up in this particular relationship—has meaning, revelation, real and dynamic import for the relation between God and *all* peoples, *men* of all peoples.

While Barth lays emphasis on the *prophetic* character of the Old Testament "as an accurate example and adequate prefiguration of the prophecy of Jesus Christ", we saw the accent in Exod. 19: 5–6 lying on the *priestly* character of Israel.

Our conclusion in regard to the universal character of the Old Testament can then read as follows: Israel has been called in her election by Yahweh to be preacher and example, prophet and priest for the nations.

The active presence of God in Israel is a sign and guarantee of His presence in the world: and the presence of Israel is thus a continuing appeal to the nations of the world.

We recall that in this chapter we are speaking only of the *universal* and not (yet) of the *missionary* character of the Old Testament. It is, however, of great significance, not only for a "theology of missions", but also for a "theology of the Church", constantly to call to mind this universal task of Israel in and for the world. In any case an introverted Church, which is tempted to consider itself the goal of the purposes of God, can never make appeal to Israel, in the light of the Old Testament kerygma.

Can an extroverted "theology of missions" do so? To this question we must seek an answer in the following chapter.

CHAPTER 2

THE OLD TESTAMENT MESSAGE OF UNIVERSALISM AS A MISSIONARY MESSAGE

1. Universalism and Mission

WHILE THERE IS BROAD AGREEMENT AS TO THE trend toward universalism in the Old Testament, great differences arise whenever one proceeds from this universalism to the *missionary* intention and commission.

In earlier years the thought of mission in the Old Testament was often seen as the end result of an extended process of development: Yahweh was assumed to have developed gradually from an Israelitic folk-god to a God of the other nations and to a world-God; the writing prophets, especially, were thought to have fulfilled an important function. Thus monotheism was thought to have had universalism as a consequence; and the idea of mission was thought in its turn to have emerged from universalism.[1]

In more recent years much criticism has been levelled against such an assumption. Some people observe monotheism already present in Moses and thus the germ of the idea of mission as well.[2] In this way the scheme of monotheism-universalism-mission continues to be maintained; and likewise the idea that the goal of the missionary idea was gradually attained. Moses has sometimes even been considered to be the first missionary.[3]

It occurs to me that the idea of this gradual ascent from polytheism via monotheism to universalism and the idea of mission can be maintained only if one assumes that the idea of mission can be gleaned from a process of growth in

29

Israel's religion. But it seems to me impossible to glean this from the Old Testament.

We are not therefore obliged to climb the ladder of polytheism-monotheism-universalism in order to come out finally at the highest rung, that of the idea of mission.

The prophetic-priestly-royal character of Israel as a people of the election is an established fact from the beginning, and it is an obsolete notion to think that the idea of a universal call could emerge only *late* in Israel. But the whole scheme of polytheism-to-monotheism-to-univer-salism-to-the-idea-of-mission is surely forced on the Old Testament, and time and again has led us off in the wrong direction. And, in particular, the idea of a postulate is surely more of a philosophical construct than an exegetical conclusion?[4] In fact, I think that if one assumes that the idea of mission is a postulate of universalism, one is up against a very great difficulty in regard to mission.

What is this difficulty? Simply this: that while the point of departure of the Old Testament is universalistic, *the idea of mission either occurs only sporadically or is missing altogether.* In this case we can call the Old Testament "missionary" only if we abandon the distinction between universalism and mission. But if we do this, we are depriving ourselves of the distinctive effort of the Old Testament. If we direct our thoughts in this chapter *exclusively* to the missionary character of the Old Testament, we will really end by considering only two portions of the Old Testament.

If *every* declaration of universalism in the Old Testament is called "missionary", then Isaiah 40–55 and the book of Jonah are indisputably the high points of the Old Testament from a missionary point of view. But if the word "missionary" is confined to the idea of being sent out to the nations with the message of salvation, then these two portions of Scripture become almost the only passages in support of an idea of mission. But even here there is no longer any unanimity because the missionary character of these passages of Scripture has not remained unchallenged.

We will want to place side by side the various views regarding these oft-discussed passages of Scripture, in order to draw our conclusions regarding the character and boundaries of the missionary message of the Old Testament.

2. The "Missionary High Points" of the Old Testament
A. ISAIAH 40–55

Almost all those who have been concerned with the question of the missionary message of the Old Testament are agreed that the universal significance and calling of Israel is nowhere expressed more clearly than here.

Those who see Moses as the *first* missionary in the Old Testament consider the author of Isa. 40–55 to have been inspired by him,[5] and thus to be continuing Moses's long-forgotten and neglected work.

Those who see the germ of the Old Testament in the divine election of Israel also recognize in Deutero-Isaiah the high point of the doctrine of election as an expression of universalism.[6]

The prophecies of universalism in Isa. 40–55 have been discussed frequently enough to render repetition of this point unnecessary.[7] The strictly *missionary* prophecies are usually confined to two Songs of the Servant of Yahweh, 42: 1–7 and 49: 1–7. It is clearly stated in these passages that the Servant is called to reveal justice to the nations (42: 1) and to be as a light to the nations (42: 6, 49: 6), in order that the salvation of God may reach to the end of the earth (49: 6). While in the remaining passages of Deutero-Isaiah it is stated only that the world of nations will be taken aback by the restoration of Israel, or that they are summoned to praise Yahweh for the liberation He extends *to Israel*, here the Servant directly calls the nations themselves to salvation.

There is pretty general agreement that the figure of the

Servant is best conceived of neither as a personification of Israel exclusively, nor as an individual person, but as a "corporate personality", who can be understood both as individual and as collective. Therefore there is real justification for speaking of a missionary calling *of Israel*. Israel is called (under the figure of the Servant) to bring justice to the nations and to be a light to the nations. Certainly the charge to mission can be formulated no more clearly, and one of the exegetes rightly observes: "The objections raised against an exegesis of Isa. 42 and 49 which imply mission activity are in my estimation valid only if we make a consistent attempt to elucidate the Servant of the Lord as an individual (and eschatological) figure."[8] This expresses the opinion of most exegetes. But quite recently there has been proposed another exegesis of these very passages. For Martin-Achard argues[9] that even in these statements regarding the Servant of the Lord the Old Testament does not go any farther than universalistic preaching; according to him there is no question here of any preaching in the world, any going out to the nations, nor of any commission to them, but only of a witness that remains confined to Israel's existence and suffering in the midst of the nations.

Let us quote Martin-Achard's conclusion concerning Isa. 42 and 49 and Deutero-Isaiah in general:

> The message of Deutero-Isaiah is not missionary in the ordinary sense of this word; his preaching does not issue in proselytism. The prophet does not invite Israel to range the world to call the heathen to repentance. The *raison d'être* of the chosen people is to exist; its presence gives testimony to the divinity of Yahweh, its life proclaims all that God is for it and for the world. The mission of Israel exists in reflecting the glory of God by accepting His gifts along with His judgments; by beholding the whole singular fortune of the chosen people, one discovers heaven and earth and their Maker. Israel exercises the function of mediator over against the nations; she points them back to Him

whom she has to thank for everything. She is their light because Israel has been lit by God's glory in a special manner. While Deutero-Isaiah preaches comfort to his brethren, he is also proclaiming that their glorious return testifies to the unique greatness of Yahweh. The marvel by which Israel lives publicizes the glory of her God to the whole world.

The fortune of the world ultimately hangs upon the existence of Israel in the midst of the nations; living by Yahweh, the chosen people lives for mankind. *That* is the missionary perspective which becomes visible in the declarations of Deutero-Isaiah.[10]

B. The Book of Jonah

Jonah, like Deutero-Isaiah, has often been termed the missionary high point of the Old Testament. It is a welcome contrast to the book of Esther (an ultra-particularistic document).

Although personally I believe that this point of view tends to exaggerate the significance of the book, at the same time it is difficult to deny that Jonah breathes an uncommonly universal spirit. But what about a missionary spirit?

Most of the exegetes are unanimous in the judgment about Jonah, too. Here, as far as they are concerned, the missionary ideal is proclaimed unambiguously, and in this book Israel is directed toward her proper calling in the world. The book is levelled against Jewish religious and nationalistic exclusivism and is thus a straight-out plea for mission among the heathen.[11] The assumption is also frequently made that the writer is dependent on the book of Deutero-Isaiah.[12]

But others, both at an earlier period[13] and more recently, deny that the book is concerned with the commission to proclaim to all nations the message of salvation. The opposition to a Jewish exclusivism consists only, according to this view, in accentuating the infinite and ample mercy of Yahweh. Martin-Achard[14] associates himself with the

33

ideas of the Roman Catholic theologian, A. Feuillet, who prefers to understand Jonah as a humiliating sermon to narrow-minded Jews; nothing more.

It cannot be denied that a real plea for mission to the heathen is lacking in the book of Jonah; at most it can only be deduced from the book.

C. AGGRAVATION OF THE PROBLEM

Now with the chief witnesses for the idea of mission in the Old Testament—Deutero-Isaiah and Jonah—no longer above suspicion, are we not led to the conclusion that we had best abandon the Old Testament as a source for the Biblical foundation of mission? Or is there still some suggestion of a common conviction in the conflicting testimony of exegesis, a conviction that can open the way to a solution of this difficult question? I believe we will do well to separate two issues.

First, it seems to me that both sides are agreed that never in the whole period of the Old Testament was there any deliberate missionary activity. Even those who hold fast to a missionary interpretation of Deutero-Isaiah and Jonah recognize that the concern is for commissions and promises which will be realized only *in the future*. During the Old Testament period no one could arrive at mission as an *act* of going out for proclamation among the nations. If the Old Testament has become acquainted with the idea of mission in the narrower sense, its realization is reserved to the future age. So we encounter the problem of the future expectation in the Old Testament.

Second, we shall do well to realize that when people use the word "mission" in contrast to "universalism" they do not always mean the same thing. At the risk of being suspected here of sophism, may I venture to complete the distinction already made between "universalism" and "mission" by a further distinction between *centripetal* and *centrifugal* missionary consciousness. I believe that those who advocate a missionary exegesis of Deutero-Isaiah and

34

Jonah are right in so far as they understand that these passages of Scripture are concerned with *more* than universalism as defined in Chapter 1. On the other hand, I believe that those who reject such a missionary exegesis are right in so far as they understand that there is no thought of mission in the Old Testament in the centrifugal sense in which it comes to the fore in the New Testament.

3. The Character of the Old Testament Expectation for the Future

The Old Testament might be characterized as the book of the expectation of Israel. The content of this expectation is none other than Yahweh Himself (Jer. 14: 8, 17: 13, 50: 7, Ps. 71: 5).

Yahweh is not, like the gods of the other nations, a power of nature, but the God of history.[15] Therefore He is almost never referred to in the Old Testament as "God of gods", as if He were the *primus inter pares* among the gods of the earth; rather He is the God of Israel. Here, and particularly here, is where His special character lies; He has entered into a covenant with men, in particular with Israel. The God of Israel is the God who steps into human life and thereby makes history. This is why history carries such a great weight in and for Israel—because it is the history of the acts of Yahweh (cf. e.g. Ps. 78, and the appeal to the acts of Yahweh in the past in the prophetic writings).

From this God, who in the past chose Israel and concluded a covenant with Abraham, everything is expected in the future as well. The Old Testament is all expectation.[16] Because Yahweh steps actively into history and leads His people, *therefore* people expect everything from Him. The past of the acts of Yahweh thus never really becomes past in the sense of finished business. The past is never *only* past; it is also a powerful witness for the active presence and power of Yahweh today, and therefore also a *promise* for Yahweh's future activity.[17]

35

In this light we must also view the relationship between Israel, as the People of God, on the one hand, and the nations (heathen), on the other.

In the past God *created* these nations. They are the work of *His* hands (Ps. 86: 9), they witness to His many-sided wisdom and goodness (Gen. 9: 16), to His yearning for peace as well (Gen. 10: 1, 32), because He blessed the earth *after* the flood with a multitude of peoples. Because the God of Israel has been the God of all nations in the past, so *also* is He in the present and will be in the future. Because the God of Israel is the Creator not only of all nations but also of heaven and earth, man and beast, therefore will He reveal Himself in the future as Creator and Possessor, and more particularly as *Redeemer* also of the whole world.

The salvation of Yahweh reaches out as far as possible in time and space (Gen. 1–11), and it will extend just as far in the future. The past is guarantee of the future and the future is confirmation of the past, because in both Yahweh is the living, the acting, and the only God.

Thus we have just as much right to say that Israel's future is defined by her past as that the appreciation of her past is defined by her expectation for the future. In the prophets' expectation for the future, and in the perspective of the Psalms, we get a new view both of creation and of the world of nations, illumined just as the description in Gen. 1–11 is illumined: by the light of the goodness, the friendship, the blessing of God.

It is precisely "to the uttermost limits of their range" that the declarations (in the Psalms and Wisdom literature) concerning creation mean to bear witness to the salvation which Yahweh will give not only as the God of Israel but as the God of all that lives and has breath (Ps. 150).[18]

People have fallen into the common habit of referring every expectation for the future to "eschatology". But it seems to me more correct to keep the word "eschatology" for that expectation of Israel which really extends to the "eschata", the farthest limits (geographical, historical, qualitative). So in general we can say that Israel's expectation of Yahweh and the God of *Israel* belongs *not* to the eschatological expectation, but Israel's expectation of Yahweh as the God of the world of nations does belong to eschatology, because here the limits are really overstepped. The sharp distinction from other nations cannot be rationalized out of the Old Testament. It would run counter to the *election* of Israel if the nations were already put on a par with Israel in the present; on the other hand, it would run counter to the *sense* and *purpose* of Israel's election if the prospect of the nations' knowing and praising Yahweh were not to be preserved in spite of the sin, the idolatry, the guilt of the nations toward Israel. But it is quite plain that He who has *made* the nations (Ps. 86: 9) and who has made them as *His* nations (Ps. 87) is also the only one who can call them to Himself. That which will bring the world of nations to Him is *not* Israel's calling them, *nor* her going out to them, but exclusively the visible manifestation of the deeds of God in and with Israel; only so will they recognize Yahweh as *their* God, i.e. confess that Israel's God is *their* God, the God of the whole earth, the *only* God.

Israel's expectation for the future in general, and *a fortiori* Israel's eschatological expectation for the nations who do not know Yahweh, the heathen, is not based on a future act of Israel's, but on the future acts of Yahweh. In other words, eschatology in the Old Testament is not concerned with a mission of Israel in the sense of a going out to the nations to preach the gospel: the mission of Israel consists in the fact that through this nation God will make His power known, visible, and tangible to the view of all nations and *with* a view to all nations.

The character of eschatology as expectation of what Yahweh will do really excludes the idea of mission in the narrower sense (Israel's going out to the nations).

37

Neither the activity of Israel nor that of the nations stands in the foreground of eschatology, but exclusively the activity of Yahweh. His acts happen *to* Israel, in the sight of the nations, and therefore *to* the nations too.

So whether there will be any deliverance directed to the nations depends upon their relation to Israel and upon Yahweh's activity in and with Israel. The arbitrariness and overweening pride of the nations (Gen. 11) prevents them from seeing reality, namely, that they have Yahweh to thank for their existence (Gen. 10); therefore He will make them see reality by creating space in their midst for a nation (Gen. 12) that is His special possession, in order to create space for His recognition among the nations. This is the theme of *Heilsgeschichte* and therefore the outlook of eschatology as well. In eschatology, *Heilsgeschichte* will find its confirmation and crown. Therefore the eschatological expectation can also avail itself of present and even of perfect (verb forms): prophetic present and prophetic perfect.

The correctness of this conception of the Old Testament expectation for the future is concisely confirmed by Karl Barth, *K.D.* IV, 3, pp. 788–92. He distinguishes between a tentative, subordinate conception, present in the foreground, of the coexistence of the nations with Israel as temptation and threat, and a conception in the background, superordinate and definitive, which sees the nations as the creation of God and as the Kingdom of God.

For our purpose here it is sufficient to establish

(i) that the expectation in regard to the world of nations is an eschatological expectation which also harks back to the past and which can therefore be celebrated—liturgically—as already present;

(ii) that the fulfilling of this expectation will be exclusively an act of Yahweh's.

4. *Mission as Eschatological Possibility*

In the light of the expectation for the future which has

been sketched out here, we must now raise the question once more as to whether there is any trace of missionary consciousness in the Old Testament or not.

Our appeal to Deutero-Isaiah, and particularly to the songs of the Servant of the Lord, is fully justified when our concern is to demonstrate the eschatological expectation for the world of nations. But we have already seen (2) that a missionary significance to these Biblical passages is both accepted (Sellin, Volz, Eichrodt, Vriezen, Rowley, Jacob)[19] and rejected (de Boer, Snaith, Martin-Achard).[20] Some go so far as to doubt or even to deny any universalistic character to Deutero-Isaiah.[21] But I must oppose such an interpretation on the ground of the unity of the Bible, and I submit that Israel's eschatological expectation of salvation becomes an expectation for the nations.[22] Likewise, I think that it is difficult to oppose the *missionary* character of such declarations as Isa. 42: 4, 45: 22, 23, 49: 6, 53: 11—for they clearly say that salvation shall reach the coastlands; that the nations shall see the light of the Servant of Yahweh, that the ends of the earth are called to turn to Yahweh.

But I think we shall have to admit that there are no compelling reasons for explaining Isa. 45: 22, 23 and 53: 11 in this way; there is no reference here to Israel's going out (or to that of the Servant of Yahweh). I do believe that this *must* be affirmed of Isa. 42: 2 and 49: 6. After all, we are doing some violence to these declarations in denying the most obvious idea in these verses, that justice shall be brought to the waiting coastlands (42: 4), and in denying that the expression "so that my salvation shall reach to the end of the earth" (in direct connection with the designation "light for the nations" of the Servant of Yahweh, 49: 6) also implies the *bringing* of the news.

Thus we must conclude that there is in fact only one statement in the Old Testament that expresses in so many words the idea of mission in the sense of "going out to the nations", and that of the other passages cited here *another*

39

interpretation is possible—simply that the nations shall *come* to salvation.

This idea is to be found not only in the passages cited here; the Psalms often express the idea that the nations shall *come* to Israel, to Jerusalem—again and again. The best known in this regard is certainly Isa. 2: 2-5 (cf. Mic. 4: 1 ff.; Zech. 8: 20, 21, 14: 16).

It is to the merit of Bengt Sundkler[23] that he has called attention to this specific form of missionary sense in Israel, namely, *the conviction that Israel and especially Jerusalem is the centre of the world, whither the nations shall turn their steps.* That this has nothing to do with the familiar ethnocentrism which is met with in so many forms throughout the world, need not be set forth in this connection in any greater detail. But it is also good to realize that the prophecy of the *coming* of the nations to Yahweh, or to Israel, Jerusalem or Zion is announced only in the later writings of the Old Testament. The notion of the universal significance of the election of Israel is certainly present from the very beginning, without, however, our having the promise of the *coming* of the nations, of the *answer* of the nations to the "universal prophecy" of Israel.

The prospect of a positive reaction on the part of the nations to the existence of Israel is first held forth in the prophetic writings and in the Psalms. To my way of thinking, this is a valid reason for distinguishing in the Old Testament between: (*a*) the thought of universalism; (*b*) the thought of mission in the centripetal sense; (*c*) the thought of mission in the centrifugal sense.

This first is quite general, and is even the very presupposition of Israel's election (Gen. 10, 11, and 12); the last is so rare that one can actually point to only one Scriptural passage with certainty, Isa. 42: 4. But the thought of mission in the centripetal sense occurs with great frequency both in the prophets and in the Psalms. By this we understand the promise of the *coming of the nations as a response to God's acts in Israel.* That Israel herself thereby fulfils the role of messenger, caller out of the land of Israel, the city of Jerusalem, or the Temple, is not out of the question. But we must certainly remember that the Psalms, for example, summon the nations to know and praise Yahweh, but that these Psalms were sung in the temple of Israel, and thus could only be heard by those there present, that is, by Israel herself.

But the execution of the summons and the promise to the nations is an affair of the future. In other words, the revealing of Israel's universal significance, the centripetal missionary function of Israel and (if necessary) the centrifugal missionary task of the Servant of the Lord (Isa. 42 : 4) is an eschatological expectation, which will be fulfilled only at the end of days.

We have paid attention here exclusively to Deutero-Isaiah rather than to Jonah (cf. 2) because of my conviction that the book of Jonah has to be classified among the universalistic and not among the missionary portions of the Old Testament. The universalism of the book of Jonah expresses anti-particularistic, anti-nationalistic, or (anachronistically) anti-Pharisaic tendencies, but I do not feel that it can be advanced as evidence for the presence in the Old Testament of a missionary commission to go outside Israel. Here, I think, we must admit, "He [Jonah] brings no new revelation regarding Yahweh, but combats a bad interpretation of Israel's election by recalling an essential characteristic of the God of Israel,"[24] namely, His care for the nations.

We will return in another chapter to another important passage in the Old Testament which in the history of revelation has fulfilled an important function, namely, Dan. 7: 1–14.

5. Summary

When, after this short survey, we inquire as to the results of our investigation into the significance of the Old Testament for a theology of mission, we must affirm, in view of

41

the present-day state of the data, that the harvest is not particularly great. When one turns to the Old Testament to find a justification and basis for missions in the current meaning, that is, as "foreign missions", one is bound to be disappointed. It does not seem advisable to build a theology of missions on a few statements, especially on those which are still exegetically in dispute.

But we may question whether there is any reason to complain about this meagre result. I certainly do not think it should be considered a loss if the Bible does not give us an answer to the questions we ask but leads our thought in another direction. It is not the human activity that stands in the foreground of the Old Testament but the divine acts for the redemption of Israel. These acts cannot be confined to Israel, for the existence and redemption of Israel has consequences for the nations. The nations do not know this themselves, it has been avowed to Israel alone; but one day it will be avowed to the nations themselves. And then the destiny of the nations will be determined in their coming to Yahweh or in their refusing to come. But this belongs to eschatological expectations, not to the promises already realized. Only in liturgy and in the visions of apocalyptic can the future be surveyed as already present.

The significance of these insights for a theology of mission becomes completely clear from the words with which Martin-Achard closes his investigation into the missionary perspective in the Old Testament:

> In conclusion, the Church cannot deny that God converts the nations, acting in the midst of His people. His intervening, and this alone, makes of Israel the light of the world. The Church evangelizes to the extent that her Lord inspires her; her existence, then, itself is her power. Mission has nothing to do with this or that political or commercial undertaking, as people have sometimes thought; it is completely dependent on the secret activity of God in the Church, it is the fruit of a life that is truly founded in God. First

42

and foremost, the evangelization of the world is not a matter of words or of activity, but of presence: *the presence of the people of God in the midst of humanity, the presence of God among His people.* It is not without purpose that the Old Testament brings this to the recollection of the Church.[25]

Now that we have distinguished the universalistic from the—in this special sense—missionary character of the Old Testament, we shall want to turn our attention in the following chapter to the connection of both these elements with the expectation of the Messiah in the Old Testament.

CHAPTER 3

THE OLD TESTAMENT MESSAGE OF UNIVERSALISM AS A MESSIANIC MESSAGE

1. Expectation of Salvation and Expectation of the Messiah

IT IS A NOTEWORTHY PHENOMENON THAT OLD TESTA-ment research in the last few decades has spent only a modest amount of effort in research into the *Messianic* character of the Old Testament in general and of the Old Testament expectation of salvation in particular.[1] Probably one reason for this is the aversion which historical criticism has always displayed for the earlier Messianic exegesis of the Old Testament on the part of the Church.[2] Another reason is that the Old Testament expectation for the future *is* always an expectation of salvation, but does not always bear the character of a Messianic expectation.[3]

The justification for calling attention here to the Old Testament Messianic expectation is that for the investigation of the Biblical foundations for a theology of mission, this Messianic expectation is, in our opinion, of special significance. Perhaps, after all, the Messiah does play a greater role than one might realize on the basis of the number of publications on the subject in recent years. It is certainly significant that Jewish and Christian traditions run parallel in regard to the explicitly Messianic passages in the Old Testament.[4]

Thus, even though future expectation and Messianic expectation may not coincide, nevertheless the Messiah is in a special sense the symbol and the culminating point for future expectation and salvation-expectation in the Old Testament. Within the limits of our investigation, we want only to trace the significance and range of the universal and missionary character of the Old Testament to the extent to which the expectation of the Messiah in Israel can fill out the picture thus far sketched.

2. Messianic Figures

A. If the Messiah figure is considered solely as a royal figure, the origin of Messianic expectation will be sought in the time of David.[5] But if not only kings, as executors of God's will, but also prophets, as proclaimers of God's will, are to be considered in a Messianic light, then the picture becomes more varied. I believe we can do justice to the Old Testament Messianic expectation only by paying attention to the prophetic as well as to the royal tradition.

In our investigation of Messianic expectation, we must further bear in mind the dynamic unity of the Old Testament and of the whole Bible, and not confine ourselves exclusively to the analytical methods of historical and literary criticism.[6]

Although with good reason Israel can be called the Messianic nation,[7] nevertheless I believe it is better to confine the term "Messianic" to those individual figures which give expression in a special way to God's will and work in history. This is not to deny that the notion of a Messiah has become compressed in the course of time and has been connected particularly with the Davidic royal house. We must certainly state emphatically that any attempts to explain the idea of the Messiah as a borrowing from other nations, particularly from Babylon or Egypt, must be regarded as a failure.[8] In the Messianic expectation, Israel's expectation for the future takes on unique form. Its origins are probably very old as we can see in the ancient sayings of Gen. 49: 8 ff., and it is not improbable that this passage contains a recollection of Gen. 3: 15, in view of the Paradise motifs which resound through it.[9, 10]

Now it is remarkable that Messianic expectation in this broader sense bears the character of universalism well-nigh continually. If, with the synagogue and early

Christian Church, we do count Gen. 3: 15 among the Messianic passages, this is simply an indication of the universality of salvation and of the Personage who brings salvation. The figure of Melchizedek, Gen. 14, interpreted Messianically in the Epistle to the Hebrews, is likewise a universal figure and its significance there is just that the universal priesthood is *more* than the Aaronic one. The same thought underlies Ps. 110 also. Perhaps here we have the key to the explanation of the remarkable fact that the priesthood in Israel seems seldom to be referred to Messianically.[11] In Gen. 49: 10, which is almost always termed "early Messianic", it is said in plain words of the Ruler of Shiloh, "to him shall be the obedience of the peoples". Here at this early stage the Messianic expectation and the expectation of universal salvation coincide completely. The Messianic statement in Num. 24: 17, is of a somewhat different character, because it is not concerned with obedience but (in harmony with the ideas of that age) with the chastisement and defeat of the nations.[12]

Also striking is the formulation in the so-called testament of David, 2 Sam. 23: 1–7, where there is no reference to a righteous ruler over Israel, but to "a righteous ruler over men". A similar nuance in such devotional sayings as these certainly has a tendency to universalism.

A similar tendency is to be found in passages which, while not explicitly Messianic, are certainly implicitly so, such as Isa. 2: 2–5, and Mic. 4: 1–4. Furthermore, beyond these we can point out other Messianic texts which see salvation dawning exclusively over Israel (Amos 9: 11, Hos. 3: 5, Isa. 4: 2—the Messianic designation "Branch" —Isa. 9: 1–6, Mic. 5: 1–5, Jer. 23: 5–8, 30: 9, 33: 14–18, Ezek. 34: 21–30, 37: 24–28, Hag. 2: 7–9, Zech. 6: 9–15), but where the designations and descriptions of the Messianic kingdom often go beyond the specifically Israelite framework. In this connection it is also not without significance that the Messiah, although almost never called "king", still receives the attributes of the general

46

style of an Oriental court outside Israel,[13] whereas this is almost never the case as regards Israel's kings themselves.

The Messiah figure is a *divine* figure who will bring to expression the actual royal lordship of God in the future. Therefore the Messiah is not so much the *bringer* and author of salvation as He is its representative. The Messiah is the visible manifestation of God Himself. In the light of this statement, all the Psalms which celebrate the future royal lordship of God belong to the category of Messianic Psalms; while, moreover, Israel's kings are often provided with Messianic features, as for example Ps. 72 *et al.* In other words, the universal lordship of God and the lordship of the Messiah are correlates: the latter is an expression of the former. *We are justified in concluding that the universal lordship of God, the eschatological expectation of salvation and the expectation of the Messiah belong together; they are, as it were, concentric circles: the Messiah is the centre of the Israelite as well as of the universal expectation of salvation.*

B. Now it is in this light that we must refer again to the well-known Songs of the Servant of the Lord. Naturally one can say that there is nothing Messianic as such in these songs;[14] but this conviction, I believe, only makes clear the fact that there is no possibility of connecting the tradition of royal Messiah expectation and the tradition of prophetic Messiah expectation.

These two traditions were probably present in Israel from early times, even though the so-called royal tradition seems to have spoken more strongly to the imagination of the nation than the prophetic. But the way the Servant of the Lord is addressed in these songs, the way he himself speaks, the way he is celebrated, point unmistakably in the direction of a Messianic figure.[15] One might rightly say that the Servant-of-the-Lord prophecies supplement and deepen the Messianic idea in ways previously unheard of:

(i) In the designation "Servant", more than in any other Messianic designation, we find an expression of the absolute surrender to the *service* of Yahweh.

47

The whole emphasis is laid on the *human* character of the Servant, which is underlined in the clearest way by his suffering and dying (Isa. 50, 53).

(ii) At the same time (Isa. 42: 1, 49: 1) his connection with Yahweh is expressed in such a way as to suggest a *more-than-human* glory and authority.

(iii) Similarly, all the emphasis falls on the establishment of the lordship of God. He magnifies the *unique* glory of God and becomes light and salvation for the world.[16]

(iv) The task of showing that Yahweh alone is God, which the other prophecies (notably Jeremiah and Ezekiel) affirm to be a task for all Israel, is here ascribed to the Servant. Through all the Old Testament historical and prophetic books we find a "progressive reduction": from the many to the few, from the nation to the remnant, from the remnant to the one Servant.[17]

If now—in contrast to our treatment in the previous chapter—we regard the Songs of the Servant of the Lord as Messianic prophecies, rather than as expressing universalism, then the question arises: do they give any further answer to our inquiry as to the missionary message of the Old Testament? The question comes to a head, I think, in another question: is the Messianic figure which appears here as the "Servant of the Lord" to be considered as a missionary personage?

If we were to confine ourselves only to Isa. 42: 4, we would certainly be inclined to answer this question affirmatively. But if we consider the four songs as one organic whole (and I think the text of the songs themselves argues very strongly for this), then we are not so sure.

Let us summarize the contents of these songs:

In the *first* song, Isa. 42: 1–7, we find celebrated the election and vocation of the Servant to be a covenant for the people and a light to the nations. The order of law, the reign of peace, and complete human well-being as a gift from Yahweh, describe a situation in which *all* the world may share.

In the *second* song, Isa. 49: 1–7, it is made clear that the fulfilling of this vocation lies *in Israel*, but seems to fail there completely. The fault for this lies not on God's side; He has given to the word of His Servant a powerfully intrusive and penetrating ability ("sword", "arrow", verses 2–4). All labour seems in vain, but the Servant is strengthened and consoled by the promise that his work for Israel will not be useless, and furthermore that he shall be a blessing, a light for *the nations*. But we are not told how this is to happen.

In the *third* song, Isa. 50: 4–9, all the emphasis falls on dedication to Yahweh and on the contumely which this means for the Servant. His message involves innocent suffering. The messenger of the righteousness of God must suffer as someone without rights.

In the *fourth* song, Isa. 53: 1–12, which bears the character of a confession by the congregation, the last and deepest secret of suffering is disclosed: innocent suffering is vicarious suffering; suffering is the way to glory, to the recompense which exists in the fact that many will be justified. It is not difficult in the light of 52: 13–15 and of the previous songs to see in those "many" a reference to the world of nations which will fall as booty to the Servant who, following death, is saved.[18]

In all the songs where there is reference to the world of nations, we do not find the Servant going out to the world of nations[19] so much as his being recompensed *by* the world of nations. In other words, the nations are the *reward* of the Messianic Servant, and the *guarantee* that his work will not be in vain. *All the emphasis falls on the fact that the world of nations is a gift to the Messianic Servant; there is no reference here to the world of nations as a "mission territory" of the Servant.* In itself it is completely understandable that we are to see these songs as mission songs, and that we see the Messiah as a Missionary. But this is not to be gleaned

49

directly from the Old Testament text. Isa. 49: 7, just as much as 52: 13–15, requires the conclusion, I believe, that the powerful acts of God with and by the Servant—which will fill the nations, and particularly the princes (the "divine" princes of the ancient Oriental world) with amazement—are the occasion *for* those princes to acknowledge Yahweh.

Here, too, if we wish to speak of the idea of mission, we must understand "missionary" exclusively in the sense of the centripetal activity of the nations; they will come to Israel in order to put themselves under the rule of Yahweh's law. This is also expressed in Zech. 8: 23: ten men from the nations of every tongue shall take hold of the robe of a Jew, saying, "Let us go with you, for we have heard that God is with you."

C. We shall want to deal separately with the important pericope Dan. 7: 1–14, and particularly with verse 14, in which the Son of Man is referred to. In another connection we shall have to return to verse 14 in more detail. We shall therefore confine ourselves here to stating the fact that it is to the Son of Man, in whom we see an apocalyptic indication of the Messiah,[20] that the dominion is *given* after it has been taken away from the four beasts. These four beasts represent kingdoms rising from the world of nations, that is, from the anti-godly depths (of the sea). Their dominion is cruel, inhuman, blasphemous, and "beastly". Over against the anti-godly powers God Himself places the power of the Son of Man.[21]

Here also the Messianic dominion over the nations is a *gift* for which neither the Messiah himself nor the nations have asked. The depicting of the dominion of the Messiah in this vision still has the special nuance of a *human* dominion, in contrast to the subhuman and brutish lords before him. All nations, peoples and tongues will enter into this dominion and will serve and obey the Son of Man (verse 14, cf. verse 27). Here also there is no reference to the *way* the nations will come to this obedient service. One can trace here a resemblance to Isa. 42: 4, 6, 49: 6, and the like, in which there *is* reference to the Messiah as the one to whom the nations look forward and for whom he shall be a light, but *not* to the way this light shall be spread and the expectation shall be fulfilled.

In the apocalyptic vision of the Son of Man, together with the figure of the Servant from the songs in Isa. 40–55, all the Messianic features which we find spread through the Old Testament are united. In regard to Dan. 7, we could set them forth as follows:

(i) The Messiah represents the Kingdom, the Royal Dominion of God; the Messiah is, as it were, the visible appearance of God Himself.

(ii) At the same time the Messiah bears "human" features, by which we do not mean to set "human" in *opposition* to "divine", but rather to indicate the *actual* divine acts really to be expected in the history of men.

(iii) This kingship he does not earn; it is granted to him on the basis of a divine intervention in the history not only of Israel but of the world of nations as well.

(iv) The Messianic dominion is a human, righteous dominion in contrast to that of the subhuman powers which have been conquered.

3. Messiah-Missionary?

In this short discussion of a few Messianic passages in the Old Testament, it has become clear that we are not being entirely fair to the distinctive nuances of the Old Testament witness if we seek bases for a theology of mission (as a "going out to the nations") in the figure of the Messiah.

The Messiah himself is more a visible appearance of God than a human figure who enters the world of nations preaching. And even where the Messiah bears expressly human features—as in the figure of the Servant of the Lord—his task is not in the first place proclamation to the nations but to Israel. Furthermore, his proclamation assumes the form of innocent suffering, a suffering that receives substitutory meaning for Israel and for the world:[22] the Lamb of God that bears the sins of the world.

The dominion over the world of nations and the obedient service to the nations falls to him, whether simply as a divine *gift* or as a reward for his innocent suffering.

Out of the world of nations itself either no activity proceeds, or else the activity is only a reaction to the eschatological-Messianic acts of God.

So it appears that the Messianic expectation in the Old Testament does add new features to the eschatological-universal expectation of the salvation of Israel, but not the missionary features which we seek as a point of departure for a theology of mission.

Thus we should again be mistaken if we concluded from the foregoing that the Old Testament is disappointing from a missionary point of view. Rather, the result we have here gained seems to me satisfying and enlarging, because the Messianic message of the Old Testament leads us to underline with special clarity what we found at the end of Chapter 2:

(*a*) That the salvation that God has promised to Israel is a *universal* salvation.

(*b*) That this salvation, as an eschatological reality, has never been received by Israel during the whole course of the Old Testament, but only expected.

(*c*) That this eschatological salvation is connected with the coming of the Messiah.

(*d*) That this universal-eschatological-Messianic salvation is not a consequence of preaching or of witness, but is a *gift* which is granted by God Himself *to* and via the Messiah.

It occurs to me that it would be good, after what has been said in Chapter 2, to bear in mind that there is no concern in the Old Testament for any human activity for the cultivation or acquisition of salvation.[23] The salvation of God for the world is a gift whose joy can be savoured in the Old Testament period only by anticipation, as hope or a firm trust in the validity and effectiveness of God's promises.

[We do not need to enlarge here any further on the fact that the word "salvation" in the Old Testament is a rendering of the word *šālôm*. Although the origin and meaning of the word is ultimately religious, it has an unmistakably material content as well. Perhaps we should say, *because* it is religious, it *also* has a material meaning. A situation of complete well-being in every respect is designated; cf., e.g. Ps. 85: 10–13, where verses 11–13 are a further definition of the *šālôm* referred to in verse 10. Remarkably enough, there is no single passage to be found in the Old Testament where *šālôm* designates an inner, personal peace or repose of mind, even though this is certainly assumed to be involved in the idea itself. The Messiah himself is thus typified in Mic. 5: 5: this is salvation, an expression which is taken over literally in Eph. 2: 14.[24]]

Perhaps it is not superfluous to return at the end of this chapter to the beginning, especially to the opinion that the Old Testament as a whole could hardly have known the idea of a personal Messiah. The question still remains whether one does not fall short of the unity of the Bible if one does not, with the ancient Church, acknowledge that the New Testament is hidden in the Old Testament, and that the Old Testament is opened up in the New.

Has Israel itself understood the Old Testament in a more Messianic sense than many Old Testament scholars do nowadays? We ask this question because it is a Christian point of view that the Old Testament is a first word which is to be explained and surpassed by a later revelation, and because for those who read the Old Testament in the light of the New there is a trend in the former towards a new and fuller revelation of God's activity. It is a remarkable fact that this pressing towards the future, this asking-for-more, appears to belong to the Old Testament in such a way that it was understood by Israel itself long before the Christian Church drew its conclusions and gave its explanation of the Old Testament.

The question which has occupied our minds in the previous chapters, namely, the question of the universal and missionary character of the Old Testament, has been clearly answered by Israel itself at a later stage of its history. Long before the missionary movement as an act of witness of the Christian Church started, Israel itself was engaged in missionary work. To be sure, we cannot overlook the fact that the missionary activity of Israel was of a different type from that of the Christian Church some centuries later; but we must not make the mistake of regarding the whole missionary activity of Israel as fanatic, nationalistic propaganda.

In its writings, too, Israel has shown a missionary mentality. For example, one may wonder whether the wisdom literature, not only outside but already inside the Old Testament, has built a bridge between a centripetal missionary consciousness and a centrifugal missionary activity. We will point out these important phenomena in the next chapter. Because we have to move partly outside the Biblical realm and also because we have to summarize still more briefly than thus far, we will call that chapter an intermezzo.

CHAPTER 4

THE INTER-TESTAMENTAL PERIOD

1. Diaspora and Proselytism[1]

IT HAS OFTEN BEEN REMARKED THAT THE NEW TESTA-
ment canot be understood merely in terms of the Old.
There is a gap of a few centuries between the conclusion
of the Old Testament canon and the beginning of the
formulation of the New Testament canon. These centuries
were of great importance to the people of Israel in regard
both to its part in and its attitude towards the world of
nations.

The diaspora greatly altered the people of Israel, and
its influence can also be seen in those who escaped it or
returned from it to the Holy Land.[2]

Here we can indicate only one of its aspects, viz. the
initiation of missionary activity among the Jews during
this period. It seems to me that this is underestimated
rather than overestimated with regard to its extent and
intensity as well as to its significance for the missionary
attitude and activity of the Christian Church in the first
few centuries of its existence.

After having investigated the proselytizing movement
among the Jews later on, Derwacter came to the following
conclusion:

> We cannot therefore give even an approximate count of
> the proselytes to Judaism in the Mediterranean world of the
> New Testament period. They were numerous enough to
> claim the attention of Philo and Josephus, conspicuous
> enough for pagan writers such as Tacitus and Horace and
> Juvenal to see them as a part of the Judaism of their time.
> They are looked upon as a factor in the great growth of the

Jewish population following the Exile. The rapid development of Christianity into a Gentile religion seems inexplicable without a large proselyte constituency. More than this can hardly be said.[2]

It cannot be said that the diaspora by itself explains Jewish missionary propaganda, but it can be said that the diaspora was its prime mover and that this propaganda was "chiefly, though not exclusively, a diaspora phenomenon".[3]

Several different elements will have to be taken into account here. Bamberger enumerates the following:[4]

(i) The decay of the Jewish nation led to greater emphasis being laid on the idea that the Jewish group was chiefly a religious entity;

(ii) The conquest of monotheism in Israel transformed Judaism into a purely universalistic religion;

(iii) The extension of the diaspora strengthened Jewish self-confidence among the colonists in new places;

(iv) Contact with other ways of thinking, and in particular with the Hellenistic, must have stimulated the Jews to undertake apologetic activities at first and missionary ones later on;

(v) The success of the Maccabean rebellion made for increased self-confidence within Palestine of a religious kind.

Long before the diaspora there had been a certain inclination towards missionary activities, as has been described in previous chapters. Accepting foreigners into the Israelitic community can rightly be considered to be a first stage, or rather a stage leading up to the Jewish mission.[5] In this connection it is particularly significant that the Hebrew word for a foreigner who has been accepted in Israel (gēr) is as a rule translated as "proselyte" in the Septuagint.[6]

G. Bertram pointed out that the diaspora cannot be completely explained by exile and emigration from the small country of the Jews.[7] Harnack estimated the number of Jews in the Roman Mediterranean area alone around the time of the birth of Christ at 4–4½ million,[8] that is about 7 % of the total population of that area. This can only be satisfactorily explained by accepting the possibility of a propagatory action. Long before the Old Testament eschatologic universalism of salvation had been deepened and extended in a missionary sense by the preaching of Christ and the apostles, the process of this reformation had been set in motion by the Judaism of the diaspora.

Study of Hellenistic Judaic missionary literature has shown how important the missionary activity must have been.[9] It was so extensive and intense that it did not at once disappear after the appearance of the young Christian Church. It is not true that Christianity has not only adopted Judaic missionary activity but has also replaced it. Until the fifth century A.D. Judaism must have continued its proselytizing activities in spite of the difficulties that increased as the Christian Church expanded.[10] And it is not only the missionary effort that must have been great, but also the *result*. In my opinion it is wrong and rather too tendentious to explain Jesus' well-known words in Matt. 23: 15, as meaning that their success must have been slight. In my opinion Bamberger's observations on this text should be considered correct and I agree with his conclusion:

> In short, this verse corroborates the testimony of Hellenistic, Roman and Rabbinic sources—that the official leaders of Judaism were eager to make converts and highly successful in achieving their aim. Distinction must be made between the highly coloured style and the actual content of the passage.[11]

More or less general agreement has now been reached with regard to the important result of Judaic missionary effort during the diaspora. The causes are partly those which Bamberger enumerated to prove the proselytizing activity of the Jews (see above). To these we could add Dalbert's remarks:

(i) The antisemitic outbursts and martyrdoms which the Jews experienced several times during the diaspora led to the growth of Judaism, just as martyrdom led later on to the growth of Christianity.

(ii) The great moral strength of Judaism, which made it superior to all pagan religions.

(iii) The strongly monotheistic tendencies in the Hellenistic world, in which the old town and state cults had often become mere formalities.

(iv) The readiness of the countries around the Mediterranean to accept spiritual values from the Orient. This orientalism, with its monotheistic tendencies and its ethical tendencies which were anchored in monotheism, gave Judaism an added attraction.

(v) The shift from Palestine legalism to the spirituality of diaspora Judaism.[12]

The great importance and influence of the Septuagint should be mentioned separately. This Greek translation of the Old Testament became—mainly through St. Paul— the great mission book of the young Christian Church, but long before that it was the Jews' mission book *par excellence*.[13] The great shift from a centripetal to a centrifugal missionary consciousness in the New Testament, which will be dealt with more fully in Chapter 6, can only be properly appreciated when viewed against the background of the translation of the Septuagint, which is much more than a mere translation—it is an exegesis and transformation of the Old Testament. This point of view will now be explained.

2. Septuagint and Proselytism

The Septuagint originated in the anxiety felt by the Jews in the diaspora that those who were living in foreign countries were in danger of losing their knowledge of the Hebrew tongue, particularly since Aramaic had taken its place as the spoken language and Hebrew retained its significance only as the language of the Holy Books.[14]

However, as soon as the Greek translation became available, it began to serve the mission. The great importance of the Septuagint certainly lay not only in *what* was in it but also in *how* the text was heard and interpreted.[15] It is certain that the fact that a diaspora had taken place had a great influence on the translation of the Hebrew text. A well-known example is the translation of Isa. 55: 5, which does not show any missionary tendency in the Hebrew text, whereas it does so very clearly in the Greek text— "Behold, thou shalt call a nation that thou knowest not, and nations that knew not thee [Israel] shall run unto thee." I have already mentioned the translation of foreigner (*gēr*) as a synonym for "proselyte". We may take it that St. Paul subscribed to a well-known interpretation when in Rom. 10: 20, he interpreted the words of Isa. 65: 1 as referring to the Gentiles, although in the Hebrew text itself no Gentiles are mentioned.[16] A similar shifting of interpretation can be noticed in the Septuagint version of Isa. 54: 15.

The fact that the Septuagint does not speak the literary language of Hellenism but the popular one of the *koine*, also gives this translation great significance from the point of view of social history; it opened the Oriental world to the Occident. According to Bertram its significance from the point of view of the history of religion is even greater.

In the Hebraic Old Testament a number of books is collected, the origin of which is extended over centuries. Therefore they reflect the manifold stages of development in the Israelitic-Judaic religion. The Septuagint comes from a much more unified world of religious ideas; it is a creation of Jewry, which owes its origin to the Persians and its world-wide activity to its Hellenistic rulers. Therefore

59

one spirit is blowing through the book; its parts fuse. Contradictions and foldings are smoothed out.[17]

An interaction took place; the diaspora developed the missionary consciousness that by implication was present in the testimonies of divine revelations and thus influenced the translation of the Septuagint, while the latter in its turn gave a vigorous impulse to missionary activity. The Jews want to be "to all mortals a guide in life".[18]

Jewish missionary effort must have been so obvious that a poet like Horace can even produce a *bon mot* about it when he wants to stress an invitation to a friend: "If you won't come willingly, we shall act like the Jews do and force you to. . . ."[19] Although one should not deduce too much from words like these, they do show that Judaic propaganda was of a particularly insistent nature. This is also evident from the extensive Hellenistic-Judaic missionary literature.[20]

If Jewish missionary consciousness is to be explained by the diaspora, Hellenism and particularly the influence of the Septuagint, one should not overlook the strong tendencies towards universalistic mission in the later parts of the Old Testament. Particularly the great importance of the later wisdom literature should be noted. It is dealt with now instead of in Chapter 2, only because it has a unique place in the canon of the Old Testament.[21]

3. Israelitic Wisdom and Proselytism

The first nine chapters of the book of Proverbs are without doubt amongst the most enigmatic and at the same time fascinating *chokma* (wisdom) literature in the Old Testament. Since this is only a survey we can discuss them only very briefly. Moreover there is still much uncertainty about the wisdom literature in general and the last word about it has not yet been said.

Israel has always known that the fear of the Lord is the beginning of wisdom. But nowhere else in the Old Testament is wisdom referred to as a *person* who is at one and the same time princeps and principle of the creation of the world. This personification of wisdom even goes to the length of representing it as a seductive woman.[22]

It is worth noting that wisdom viewed in this way becomes important from the point of view of the history of the world and the history of salvation. Israel is not the only nation to possess wisdom; the world of nations possesses it too. "By me kings reign, and princes decree justice. By me princes rule, and nobles, even all the judges of the earth" (Prov. 8: 15, 16).

This should probably be interpreted as meaning, not that Israel's particular role in God's saving activity is denied, but that this divine wisdom is rightly known and recognized only in and by Israel as the first of Yahweh's creatures.[23]

Seen against the background of the way of thinking of the Old Testament, it nevertheless remains a remarkable phenomenon that the share the nations have in divine wisdom is spoken of here without reference to Israel's unique position and significance, at any rate without the election of Israel being directly mentioned and referred to.

In Prov. 8: 35, the normal order of the Old Testament is even reversed. The gods of the nations are idols and nonentities; only Israel's God is the living and life-giving God. Here, however, it is not said that he who finds Yahweh also finds Life, but the other way round; he who finds wisdom, finds life and so Yahweh's favour—"For whoso findeth me (=Wisdom), findeth Life, and shall obtain favour of the Lord". What else does this mean but that wherever there is wisdom, Yahweh is present?

In later days this Wisdom will be identified more particularly with the Torah. This does not deny its universal significance but it does give it a more disguised, Judaic character. One has only to compare Prov. 1–9 with statements regarding the wisdom of Ecclesiasticus and the Wisdom of Solomon.[24] The word that awakens man to life and salvation is the same as that which God used as a plan when creating the world.[25]

Those curious chapters 1–9 of Proverbs are, as it were, a bridge between Israel and the nations. The way of thinking in these chapters is more or less the same as that in the first eleven chapters of Genesis. That which was meant in the latter as Israel's credo, sounds in the former like an appeal to anyone who is willing to listen, be it within or outside Israel; the salvation of the world lies in the wisdom that was already present when the world began.

This way of thinking reveals a positive attitude towards the world of nations and the fact that this positive attitude was evidently legitimate in Israel and was even sanctioned by the Judaic canon should warn us to be careful when we judge Israel's "exclusivism" or "particularism".

And if Prov. 1–9 came into being in the post-exile period, then it is certainly also thanks to this wisdom literature that Israel became more and more aware of its missionary calling. It is not to be wondered at that in the old Christian Church personified Wisdom was looked upon as a prefiguration of Jesus Christ. Did He not Himself make use of this wisdom if not identify Himself with it when He said, in words borrowed from the *chokma*: "Come unto me, all ye that labour and are heavy laden, and I will give you rest. Take my yoke upon you, and learn of me; for I am meek and lowly in heart: and ye shall find rest unto your souls. For my yoke is easy, and my burden is light"? (Matt. 11 : 28–30, cf. Ecclus. 51 : 23–27, 6: 24–30.)

We should certainly not attach too much importance to Prov. 1–9; in careful hermeneutics one should never promote a surprising and rare perspective in the Old Testament to the level of a general and guiding point of view. On the other hand, while searching for the spirit and intention of the Scriptures, one should not neglect this testimony either. It seems to me that so far the wisdom literature has not received the attention it deserves, particularly in missionary science.

In the apocalyptic of the Old Testament and particularly in the book of Daniel we find a connection between wisdom and apocalyptic; wisdom also gives insight into the secrets of the future (Dan. 2: 31, 4: 6, 5: 12, 7–10 *passim*). This can easily be understood, because apocalyptic, like *chokma*, is of a universal nature, though in a different sense from the other parts of the Old Testament.

If we now go on to discuss the data to be found in the New Testament we should remember that it not only builds on those parts of the Old Testament that are accounts of history and prophecy, but is also a reaction to the chokmatic and apocalyptic statements which used to play such an important part in the life and thoughts of post-exile Israel, amongst those who were in diaspora as well as amongst those who still lived in Israel itself, particularly in the centuries following upon the conclusion of the Old Testament canon.

It has been established that the missionary consciousness of the early Christian Church is partly due to these centuries which are not mentioned in the Old Testament itself.[26]

We are now faced, however, with the extremely awkward question whether this Christian missionary consciousness is indeed a continuation and strengthening of *Judaic* missionary consciousness. So far the terms proselytism and missionary activity have been used indiscriminately in this chapter. There is a tendency to separate these two ideas sharply. In the present circumstances this is unavoidable as well as healthful.[27]

Can the Judaic propaganda of the post-exile period *in its entirety* be called proselytism in the derogatory sense which the word nowadays has? Or should Matt. 23: 15 be seen as a protest against the *excesses* of an originally legitimate missionary impulse?

A study of the data in the New Testament will show that the missionary consciousness of the Christian Church did not fall from the air but that, on the other hand, one should be very careful about continuing the line from Judaic missionary propaganda to the Christian Church. A distinction will have to be made between the apostolic statement that "if any man be in Christ he is a new creature" (2 Cor. 5: 17) and the activities of the Christian Church that were not *only* determined by its "being in Christ".

In this study, the main aim of which is to report the data to be found in the Bible, the question of the connection between the Old Testament and the New and the difference between the Old Testament and the New will be dealt with apart from the question of how far Christian mission and Judaic proselyte activity were related genetically and historically. It seems to us that this question is mainly of importance from the historical point of view. It is therefore outside the scope of this study, although in our opinion it had to be mentioned in this chapter, which is intended as an intermezzo.

CHAPTER 5

THE NEW TESTAMENT MESSAGE OF UNIVERSALISM IN RELATION TO THAT OF THE OLD TESTAMENT

1. Introduction

THE IMPORTANCE FOR A THEOLOGY OF MISSION OF having a true insight into the message of the Old Testament is obvious from the difficulties which people have had with various passages of the New Testament dealing with the Gentiles. We are referring here specifically to the problem of Jesus and mission, Jesus and the Gentiles, which has set many pens going in the course of the years.[1] Only by a clearer insight into the structure and intention of the message of the Old Testament could a satisfying solution to this problem be found, which—except for details—has been fairly generally accepted, at least in missionary circles.

In this chapter we want particularly to underscore the continuity of the Old and the New Testaments in regard to the questions with which we are here concerned. It is perhaps not superfluous to point out that continuity is quite different from identity. Over against the tendency in theology which lays strong emphasis on *continuity*—the inclination to view the New Testament as only an appendage to the Old Testament—we wish to affirm emphatically that the message of the New Testament brings us something quite *new*, and by the glow of this new thing not only does the old pale, but it is replaced by something that is more than just the fulfilment of the old expectations. In fulfilment, the expectations are not only exceeded but also overtaken, modified, corrected. And over against the other tendency to pay too little attention to the great significance of the Old Testament for the New Testament, we wish to affirm just as emphatically that the "new" in the New Testament is nothing else than that which had already been predicted in the Old Testament, and it is of great significance that the "new" in the New Testament is illuminated and clarified time and again from the Old Testament, so that we go off on the wrong track if we neglect the Old Testament as irrelevant.

It thus seems to me of essential importance for the construction of a theology of mission that both the unity and the diversity of the Old and New Testaments be kept in mind, because the diversity can be understood *rightly* only from the unity, and the unity receives its *full* significance *from* the diversity. Particularly in respect to the idea of "mission" must these things be kept firmly in mind, because the New Testament brings us something totally new which is quite lacking in the Old Testament: the commission to proclamation to the nations, to mission in the centrifugal sense. We would do scant justice to the New Testament witness were we to see this only as a victory over or as a contrast to the Old Testament witness. On the other hand, it seems to me fully as much an impoverishment and a misjudgment of the great significance of the call to mission if we explain the centrifugal commission only as a *form*, or a mode, of the centripetal task.

In this chapter we want to show, in the first place, that great continuity exists between the Old and the New Testament witness with respect to the nations, in order to indicate, in the second place, the differences from the Old Testament which will prevent our confusing continuity with identity. In particular we shall have to indicate the progression of *Heilsgeschichte*, which offers surprising new perspectives as well.

In this chapter we shall confine ourselves chiefly to the witness of the Gospels. In the next chapter we shall concentrate on the call to mission proper, as the completely new element that distinguishes the New Testament from the Old Testament. That this "new" has roots in the "old" will then be set forth. Then, besides the so-called "great commission", the letters of Paul and the other writings of the New Testament will claim our attention. In the final chapter we shall try to find an answer to the question as to how, in the light of study of the Old Testament and the New Testament, and in the light of the present-day situation in missions, a "theology of mission" is to be constructed.

2. *Jesus, Israel, and the Nations*

A. Earlier exegetes could not deny that Jesus avoided a mission to the Gentiles, though they affirmed that Jesus would have expressed Himself in *favour* of a mission to the Gentiles, or would have pursued it Himself; and it is now seen to be an incontestable fact, which the Gospels state clearly, that Jesus consciously wished to confine His activity to Israel. We find the clearest statement in Matt. 15: 24: "I was sent only to the lost sheep of the house of Israel." That Jesus spoke of the "house" to a woman who did not belong to the house of Israel at all is an added bit of evidence that Jesus kept the contrast firmly in mind between Israel and the world of nations, quite in accord with the Old Testament doctrine of election. Israel is God's vineyard (Mark 12: 1 ff.), God's flock (Matt. 10: 6), and the promises of God are valid particularly for Israel: the Kingdom of God will be granted to Israel (Matt. 8: 12, Luke 12: 32).[2]

Over against this, the Gentiles (the nations) are drawn in the same dark colours which we have already seen in the Old Testament: they do not know God, but they camouflage that ignorance in their prayers by verbosity (Matt. 6: 7), they seek only the things of this world (Matt. 6: 32, Luke 12: 30), they can act only contrary to God (and His Messiah) (Mark 10: 33, Luke 21: 24, cf. Acts 4: 27).

67

He forbids His disciples emphatically: "Go nowhere among the Gentiles, and enter no town of the Samaritans, but go rather to the lost sheep of the house of Israel" (Matt. 10: 5-6). His judgment on the missionary zeal of the Jews is completely annihilating (Matt. 23: 15).[3]

It will not do to soften the weight and keenness of these passages by appealing to the fact that Jesus did heal and preach outside Israel as well, because in neither case was there any concern for a labour of mission among the Gentiles by Jesus Himself: the healings of Matt. 15: 21-28 and Matt. 8: 5-13 take place from afar; and His crossing the Jewish borders was done for the sake of the Jewish population in previously Jewish areas rather than directed to the Gentiles.[4]

B. Attempts to ascribe this state of affairs to Jesus' nationalism or "particularism" have now been almost completely abandoned. We recognize all this—and I believe correctly—as a sign that Jesus kept Himself within the "historic context of revelation".[5]

This context also implies that salvation for the Gentiles was expected at the time of the end, when God's Kingdom would be fully revealed in Israel. That Jesus considered this time of salvation as immediately near, and that He brought it into connection with His own Messianic commission, appears convincing in all the Gospels. In no way does He give in to the nationalistic feelings of aversion and hate, as we can see from His attitude toward the Samaritans and His parable of the good Samaritan (John 4, Luke 9: 51 ff., 10: 25-37, 17: 11-19), in which respect He runs counter to prevailing attitudes (Luke 4: 16-30).[6]

At the last judgment, Israel as well as the world of nations will stand before God, and *Gentiles* as well as Israelites will be saved and be lost (Matt. 25: 31 ff.), and *many* Gentiles will share in the fellowship of God at the end of days (Matt. 8: 11, 12: 41 ff.). Belonging to Israel is no guarantee at all of protection against God's judgment (Matt. 3: 9, Luke 13: 6-9): on the contrary, the differ-

68

ences between Israel and the nations will then fall away (Luke 13: 1–3, Matt. 23: 37) and Israel will have more to answer for than the Gentiles (Matt. 12: 41 f., Luke 4: 25–27).[7]

Jesus' promise of salvation to the nations, however, becomes fully clear only if we see it in the light of His Messianic declarations. We must consider here, first, the self-designation "Son of Man", which is borrowed from Dan. 7: 13. It is a Messianic title which indicates universal dominion, though it also probably serves to *hide* Jesus' Messianic character during His ministry through Israel. For Jesus is so completely different from the Messiah of Jewish nationalistic expectation.[8] But it has been demonstrated beyond doubt that the Son-of-Man title is certainly intended to reflect the universal claims and the eschatological character of Jesus' Messianic commission,[9] which first becomes fully clear during the trial before Caiaphas and *after* the resurrection.[10]

In the second place, we must make reference to the appropriation by Jesus—not explicitly by *name*, but certainly by His work—of the "Servant of the Lord" figure in Isaiah (Matt. 12: 15–21, Mark 10: 45).[11] By this means His work, His suffering, and His dying are explained as a suffering and dying for the "many" (Mark 10: 45, 14: 24), in which, by universal consent, we are to see a designation of the world of nations.[12]

In the third place, the claim to the title "Son of David" must, in the light of Ps. 110, be seen as an indication of the world dominion of Jesus as Messiah (Mark 12: 35–37).[13] The account of Jesus' entry into Jerusalem on an ass instead of on a royal horse, Mark 11: 1–10, is also obvious in this connection. This strange entry must be considered in direct connection with the dominion of peace over all nations: Zech. 9: 9 f., cf. Isa. 9: 4–6.[14]

Among the parables of Jesus are several which point to a salvation for *all* nations. The well-known Old Testament image of the pilgrimage of the nations to Jerusalem and

of the feast of the nations at the end of the times (Isa. 2:
2–4, 25: 6–8) recurs in various statements and parables of
Jesus. Jeremias[15] has stated in a few sharp lines "what
Jesus read in His Bible about the eschatological pilgrimage
of the nations to the mount of God". In these, according
to him, five features are to be distinguished: (a) the
epiphany of God (Isa. 51: 5, Zech. 2: 11, Isa. 2: 2, 51: 4,
60: 3, 62: 11); (b) the summons of God (Ps. 50: 1, Isa. 45:
20, 22, 55: 5, 66: 19, Ps. 96: 3, 10); (c) the march of the
nations (Isa. 2:3, 19:23, Zech. 8: 21, Jer. 3: 17, Ps. 47: 9)
laden with gifts (Isa. 18: 7, 60: 5–20, Hag. 2: 7, Ps. 68:30,
32); (d) the worship in the sanctuary of the world, Jerusalem (Isa. 56: 7, 66: 18, Isa. 45: 14, 24, Ps. 22: 27, 72:
9–11, 86: 9, Zeph. 3: 9); (e) the feast on the mount of the
world, Zion (Isa. 25: 6–8).

Like Sundkler, Jeremias also accentuates the centripetal character of the image in both the Old Testament
and the Gospels.[16] This presentation of the pilgrimage of
the nations lies at the basis of the well-known statement in
Matt. 8: 11. Jeremias rightly refers to Isa. 49: 12 and Isa.
25: 6,[17] and remarks that it is from this image that we
must explain all the eschatological parables and passages
which have reference to the feast.[18] Closely related to the
image of the pilgrimage of the nations is that of a gathering
of the flock (Matt. 25: 31 f., John 10: 16, 11: 51 ff.), and
that of the temple (Mark 11: 17, 12: 10, 14: 58, John 12:
20 ff.),[19] that of the city on a hill (Matt. 5: 14),[20] the light
on the stand (Matt. 5: 15, Mark 4: 21, Luke 8: 16, 11:
33), the stream of life (John 7: 37), the inheritance (Matt.
25: 34), and the tree wherein the birds of the air make
their nests (Matt. 13: 32). In *all* these images we find the
same concern as in the image of the pilgrimage of the
nations, namely, that of universal and eschatological
salvation.[21] Although this conclusion would appear at first
sight to many somewhat strange, and reminds us of the
eschatological dream out of which Karl Barth would like
to awaken men,[22] it must be admitted on the other hand

that *the frequently used concept of the Kingdom of God, or of Heaven,* always *includes the world of nations.* And from *this* statement—irrefutable, I believe—it certainly becomes probable that we must understand the images and parables in the New Testament in this light of universal salvation.

The question arises, why has Jesus separated His task for Israel so strictly from His expectation for the nations? The answer we shall give is twofold: (1) Salvation must first be offered to Israel before the Gentiles (the nations) can be received into the people of God. In this light we must understand, too, Jesus' strong prohibition to the disciples against going to the Gentiles, Matt. 10: 5–6: the Kingdom of God *is* at hand, but its eschatological revelation has not yet come. (2) The Kingdom of God can dawn only after the blood of the true Passover Lamb has been shed (Isa. 53: 11, Mark 10: 45, 14: 24).[23]

C. Now we come to the point where we must make clear the fact that *continuity* between the Old Testament and the New Testament does not mean *identity*, but includes *difference* as well. So long as we view the eschatological expectation of salvation in the Old Testament as the only possible sort of expectation of salvation we can do no justice to the witness of the New Testament.[24]

The view is steadily gaining ground that when one has stated the continuity between the Old Testament eschatology and the message of the Gospels, one has still said only the first word as regards the distinctive character of New Testament eschatology.

This distinctive character must be described as follows: with the coming of Jesus as the Messiah, and with the coming in Him of the Kingdom of God (Mark 1: 14–15), we still have only a provisional fulfilment of the promises made to Israel during the period of the Old Testament.

We must therefore review the significance of this tension between the fulfilment *and* the provisional nature of the Messianic Kingdom of God which has come in Christ. In other words, we must demonstrate the progression and unfolding of the *heilsgeschichtlich* activity of God, as this is proclaimed to us in the New Testament in contrast to (but not in opposition to) the Old Testament perspective, in so far as it is of importance to us in our investigation of the Biblical foundation and motive of mission.

3. *The Kingdom, the Apostles, and the Church*

A. The theme and contents of the Gospel are the proclamation of the Kingdom of God as a fulfilment of the Old Testament promises.[25] Its actualization begins in the preaching of Jesus.[26] In His preaching the Messianic character of the coming Kingdom of God comes into sharper focus than could be expressed in the Old Testament. For the relation between the Kingdom of God and the Messianic revelation becomes a *correlation*, of such force that one can almost speak of an *identification* of Jesus Christ and the Kingdom of God; He not only *proclaims*, but He *is* in His person the Kingdom which is at hand.

We can see here the first contrast between the Old Testament expectation and the New Testament fulfilment. Not only is the *expectation* of salvation in the Old Testament being fulfilled; the *revelation* of salvation is becoming clearer, because the *history* of salvation (*Heilsgeschichte*) is unfolding. In close connection with these facts is the following:

The Messianic self-declarations of Jesus undoubtedly contain the *universal* dominion of God. Although He knows Himself to be the Messiah of Israel, and as such has chosen the way of suffering and crucifixion, He has not only steadfastly rejected the designation "Messiah", but He has also led the thoughts both of His disciples and of those who rejected Him in another direction. This is clear from His plain preference for the appellation "Son of Man", a name which occurs in the Gospels exclusively as a *self*-designation of Jesus. The writers of the Gospels apparently mean to say that the universal-Messianic consciousness was present in Jesus, but that neither friend nor foe understood its range before the work of Jesus had received its fulfilment in cross and resurrection. Jesus opposes the *expectations of a narrowly Israelite sort* (coloured in part by nationalism) by opening out *prospects of universalism*. Aside from the title "Son of Man", this fact also becomes clear in the preaching of Jesus, particularly in the parables which reveal their secret only if we understand them as signs of the eschatologically universal Kingdom of God.

It is this eschatological character of the parables which opens our eyes to the fact that that magic word "eschatological" has not said everything. For precisely in these parables we see that the coming of Jesus does not mean *the absolute end*, but rather that it ushers in *a new period* in the history of Israel and of the world. This is the third point of distinction between the Old Testament expectation and the New Testament fulfilment. And it is just *this* distinction which is of all-determinative significance for a true understanding of the missionary call which Christ has given to His Church. For while the gospel is the fulfilment of the expectation of salvation, that fulfilment still bears a tentative character, and becomes in itself the source of a new expectation.[27]

[This new expectation is often interpreted as applying to the near future, and there has also been talk of a delay in the Parousia, the Second Coming of Christ, which was (according to this view) the cause of great disappointment for the early Christians.[28] Others have been of the opinion that the expectation for the near future played a smaller role than has generally been assumed, and some even want to deny any meaning at all to eschatology after cross and resurrection.[29] Still others are of the opinion that the resurrection of Christ is really to be put on the same level with the Second Coming.[30] Our belief is that these ideas do not do justice to the actual contents of the Gospels, and that we must recognize that the New Testament witness concerning eschatology cannot be brought under one denominator. We must distinguish, I believe, between at least three data which are not mutually exclusive but which supplement and clarify each other: (a) the coming of Jesus is indeed the fulfilment of the Old Testament expectation for the future and to that extent is a complete, unambiguous, eschatological event;[31] (b) the coming of Jesus, and especially His suffering and resurrection, ushers in a new age in which it becomes clear that the revelation of the Messiah does mean the end of a *particular* period of salvation, but not the end of the times;[32] (c) the end of the times remains, or rather becomes an object of future expectation in which the complete breakthrough of the Kingdom of God is connected with the Second Coming of Christ.[33]

Item (a) has already claimed our attention in §2 of this chapter. Now we must turn to the meaning of (b) and (c).]

In this connection the parable of the sower (Matt. 13 and parallels) is of much significance since it forms "in many respects the point of departure and the basis for an understanding of the ensuing parables".[34] This parable is concerned with "the connection between the event painted in the parable and the revelation of the Kingdom of Heaven".[35] The Kingdom of God (which has come in and with Christ) now goes the way of the seed, and the Messiah assumes the figure of the Sower. In the great eschatological hour of fulfilment, this is just what is happening: "a sower goes out to sow—nothing more; and that means a new world of God".[36] This Kingdom will fare just as the seed does: there are failures but there is also (and even in a wonderfully abundant way) fruit. The salvation of God has come, and as a seed. *This assumes time and space to grow and ripen to the harvest.* The same thought lies at the basis of the parable of the tares among the wheat, Matt. 13: 24–30, 36–43, in which, even more clearly than in the previously considered parable, *time as a factor within the Kingdom* emerges: "Whoever sows cannot

74

forthwith mow."[37] In the parable of the net, Matt. 13: 47–50, there is a similar concern for the distinction and the interval between gathering and separating and sorting.[38] We are to view in the same way the parables of the seed growing secretly (Mark 4: 26–29), of the mustard seed and the leaven (Matt. 13: 31–33). The sense of these parables is obscured just as much by a one-sidedly present concept of the Kingdom as by an exclusively future one.[39]

At the same time, we must recognize the coming of the Kingdom and the delay of the end—as a special gift of the Messianic time. There is an interval of time between the revelation of the Kingdom of God and the Last Judgment, an interval which becomes the great characteristic of the Messianic self-revelation of Jesus. Jesus is Saviour *before* He is Judge. The parables of the Lost Sheep, the Lost Coin, and the Prodigal Son (Luke 15) must also be understood in this light. The divine power and glory which are granted to the Messiah can be exercised by Him only in the restricted way which God has indicated to Him. This way is *the way of vicarious suffering and dying*. The Son of Man is also the Servant of the Lord. It is both foci which together determine the content of the Gospel.[40]

"The teaching and work of the historical Jesus are only to be understood in the light of His consciousness of fulfilling the role of the suffering Servant of God and that of the returning Son of Man."

"In the performance of these two tasks—as suffering *Servant of God* and as the *Son of Man* who is to return on the clouds—Jesus has fulfilled God's plan of salvation. The suffering Servant of God has fulfilled the purport of the history of the people Israel, which lies enclosed in substitution . . . ; the Son of Man, coming on the clouds, completes God's work of creation as the Man, the Second Adam, at which the creation (*Erschaffung*) of man, made in the image of God, has aimed."[41]

In the vicarious suffering and death of Christ there lies a strong motive for the delay in the judgment of the world.[42] Therefore His resurrection does not mean the end but the beginning of a new period in world history. For the forgiveness and reconciliation accomplished through it already carry within themselves the character of judgment. By Christ's suffering, judgment is not only postponed but in a certain way it is taken over and borne by *Him*. In Him the possibility is now open to escape the judgment. But *then* there must be preached to all nations also what Christ has done vicariously, for Israel (by the Son of Man, who is the Servant of the Lord) and for the whole world (by the Servant of the Lord, who is the Son of Man). Jesus Himself appears to be the seed which dies (John 12), but which will also bear fruit. This fruit, however, needs a time of ripening, and a time for bringing in the harvest—which shall be abundant, because it is the harvest of the whole world. Here the *assumptions* and *motives* of *the preaching of the Gospel to the nations* are disclosed. It is this *Messianic way* of the seed, suffering and dying, of the resurrection thereafter, and of the preaching of the Gospel among the nations, that is the new element through which the fulfilment far surpasses the expectation. God's eschatological activity in Christ opens out a most surprising perspective, the surprising thing being not the *fact* of the coming of the nations, but *how* they come, and the *condition* for their coming.

There is thus good reason to speak of a "dethronement" of eschatology[43] in the message of the New Testament, because the "last things" which have been enacted in Christ are at the same time the "first things" of a new age and of a new world. This does not mean that we are eliminating eschatology as no longer relevant. On the contrary, it means that instead of an end-point on the timeline of history we have a *line* which points toward a further and definitive end-point.

From all this discussion, we may conclude that even "the coming of the nations" is not enacted at a point of time but is stretched out over the full length of history.

This history is to be characterized as the time of sowing and growing *before* the harvest, the time of the throwing of the net, the time of the gathering of the fish *before* sorting, the time of the working of the leaven in the meal, and therefore *also* a time of patience, watchfulness, perseverance and expectation. It is not eschatology itself, but a *wrongly understood* eschatology, which contains the danger.[44]

B. The picture here sketched of the Kingdom of God as the end-point of the Old Testament expectation and as the point of departure for the dawning of a new era for the nations, is further clarified if we ask ourselves what significance the apostles have in the new situation. Current discussions of the "apostolate" direct our attention to the apostles and to their function in the Kingdom of God. Here, too, we must confine ourselves to suggesting the lines which are of importance for our subject.[45]

First of all, it must be established that the word "apostle" in derivation and meaning, is not "missionary" in the sense we usually ascribe to it. In this regard, the use of the word "apostolate"—if we intend the meaning "missionary" in the ordinary sense—indicates a significant alteration of meaning in comparison with the New Testament usage. The word is derived from the juridical rather than the theological world, and means: to be fully entrusted with the responsibility or representation of another; that is, a mandatory or a "principal", in the legal sense in England (the Dutch word is *lastgever*). That this word is not to be considered an equivalent of "missionary" or "one sent" (although the literal meaning of the Greek word does suggest this) appears from the fact that Jewish missionaries at the time of Jesus are never called "apostles" (Hebrew *šelûhîm*).[46] The apostles are those authorized by Jesus, whose significance for the first Christian community consists particularly in the fact that they are witnesses of the resurrection, and clothed by Jesus personally with the authority of witnesses. From this alone follows

77

their missionary vocation. Although the twelve apostles do not represent the New Testament apostolate *exclusively*,[47] the concept of "apostle" *is* certainly defined by them, by the twelve chosen by Jesus. This group of twelve represents Israel first of all, in particular the twelve tribes of Israel. They form the beginning, the nucleus of the eschatological people of God around the Messiah[48] (Matt. 19: 28) and *thus* they are also sent out to the lost sheep of the house of Israel (Matt. 10: 5-6).[49]

Here, too, we see how Jesus' appearance as Messiah remains within the bounds indicated by the Scriptures.[50] But the vocation and task of the apostles is seen to be a future one (Matt. 18: 18, cf. 16: 19). While Jesus Christ brings the great Messianic future He, at the same time, opens a new future for His own. The particular work of the apostles must thus also wait; on them is laid a provisional silence (Matt. 16: 20) which will be broken only by a sign from Jesus Himself (Acts 1: 8). Only as the Messianic sacrifice has been made does the commission given by Jesus to the disciples come into full activity. And *then*, for the first time, all boundaries may (and must) be crossed to proclaim the salvation of the Kingdom through all the earth. Only *after* the resurrection does the title "apostle" take on the special overtone of "missionary", one sent to the uttermost parts of the earth. To do justice, then, to the word "apostle", we must distinguish three meanings:

   (i) Proxies of the Messiah, who in His name proclaim and demonstrate the salvation of the time of the end (by healing the sick, etc.);

  (ii) First-fruits and representatives of the Messianic people of the time of the end;

 (iii) Witnesses of His resurrection to the uttermost parts of the earth, who carry on the work of Christ in the world (John 17: 18, 20: 21).

In other words, the eschatological task and position makes them both the first-fruits of the new age and a new people of God. Continuity with the Old Testament is maintained but it is equally clear that the position of the apostles is not identical with that of the twelve tribes in the Old Testament. *The progression of Heilsgeschichte which is here found continues, in that the "last of the days" does not mean the end of the days, but a great turning of the days toward a new future.*

C. From the apostles to the Church is but one step. For the Church must be built on the foundation of the apostles and prophets (Eph. 2: 20). She is the new community of the Messiah of which the apostles are the beginning. Descent from Abraham is not determinative in her (Matt. 3: 9), nor is belonging to Israel (John 8: 37–40, cf. Gal. 3: 29, Rom. 4: 16–17), but only the faith and works of Abraham (cf. Gal. 3: 28)—and these can exist only in so far as one acknowledges the Messiah of Israel and rejoices with Him in the salvation of the nations (John 8: 56).

This community of Christ, going out from the centre (the apostles), will reveal itself in the world as the people of the time of the end, the flock of the good Shepherd (John 10), the real Israel (cf. 1 Pet. 2: 10).

Nowhere in the New Testament is the Church made the equivalent of the Kingdom of God, but neither is the one set anywhere in opposition to the other. The Church is the community gathered around Christ and gathered by Christ (and by the apostles who are proxy for Him). She is not herself the Kingdom, but she is its manifestation and its form. The Church herself is a sign of the new future which has broken in for the world. It is true that the Church made her appearance as a result of the expectation of the Kingdom of God, but only in the sense that she has taken this expectation into herself. The Christological character of the Church does not exclude her eschatological character, but includes it. In other words, the Church is the "holy, catholic, apostolic Church" only when she receives the eschatological expectation of the fullness of the Kingdom. If she does *not* do that, then the great ques-

79

tion is whether she has the right any longer to be called the community of the Kingdom and of the King.[51]

If this confession of the Church *as the form and anticipation of the Kingdom of God* is correct, then it implies that the Church has substituted for the Old Testament's "not yet" the "already", though this "not yet" of the Old Testament is not dropped. So one might really express the situation of the Old Testament and of the New Testament in this way: "not yet"—"already"—"not yet".

In regard to the world of the nations, this means that the Church, in so far as she has taken the place of Israel, represents the salvation which has come in Christ, just as in the Old Testament, Israel could, in anticipation, represent the salvation of the world. But the difference is that the Church no longer merely anticipates, she remains a symbol of the hopes for the Kingdom in the fullness of the nations.[52] *Mission* comes into view when this hope for the world takes the form of *acts* of proclamation on behalf of Christ.[53]

At this point we make the transition to the following chapter. We have wanted to emphasize the *continuity* of the Old Testament and of the New Testament witness, in the progression and modification of *Heilsgeschichte*. In the next chapter we want to go further into the whole new and surprising aspect of the New Testament witness, namely, the summons to mission among the nations. Only now, therefore, do we come to a discussion of the Biblical bases of mission in the strict and only sense of the word. Yet how can one distinguish and evaluate the "new", if he does not know the "old"?

CHAPTER 6

THE MISSIONARY MESSAGE OF THE NEW TESTAMENT IN CONTRAST WITH THE OLD TESTAMENT

1. Presuppositions

IN TURNING OUR ATTENTION TO THE MISSIONARY commission as it is given us in the New Testament we want first of all to set down the conditions and presuppositions which have led to this missionary commission.

(1) In the first stage of the history of the world, God is creator of heaven and earth; He grants life and peace to man *after* (and even in) his disobedience, and He reveals something of His manifold divine wisdom in the multitude of nations (Gen. 10). At the same time, He resists the attempts of man to give form to his life and future himself without acknowledging God as the Lord over his life. This divine resistance leads to the scattering of the nations over the whole world, as a sign and consequence of the fellowship men had had and have now lost.

In this divine judgment (which must be fully recognized as judgment, just like the deluge and the expulsion from the Garden of Eden), the way is opened to a restoration of fellowship between God and man, and thus between God and the world of nations—this way is the election of Abraham.

(2) At this point history enters a new phase, that of "one for many": Abraham the individual from Ur, Israel the individual among the nations, but also a witness to all nations that God has not abandoned the world but continues His work. Further, when Israel defends herself against the nations, it is only a defence against *apostasy*;

when Israel suffers *by* the nations, it is a suffering for God's sake. When Israel forgets the distinction between herself and the nations, she commits treason not only against the covenant of God but also against those nations for whose sake she has been set apart.

But the failure of Israel as the Servant of the Lord will not prevent God from reaching the goal He envisages for the future; He *will* reach it. The expectation of Israel is concentrated in the expectation of the coming Kingdom over the nations, represented in the expected Messiah. World history is a history around Israel, just as Israel's history is a history around the works of God. The victory and the justification in the judgment of the God of Israel over against the nations and their gods is the final goal and the great prospect of history. Therefore the revelation of the salvation of God means both the redemption of Israel and the liberation of the nations. "How" these nations will share in salvation remains unsaid; but the "that" is incontrovertibly established.

(3) The third stage of history begins with the coming of Jesus Christ. With Him the Kingdom of God pushes its way through: the last phase, the end of days has come. In Him is manifested the *ultimate* intention of God with Israel and with the world: He will bear the judgment Himself and open the way to salvation for all. The "last of days" thus becomes a new beginning. The time of eschatological expectation is past, the time of eschatological fulfilment has dawned. But the fulfilment is just at the early stage; therefore the expectation remains part of life and even determines life. In this tension of the "already" and the "not yet", *all* the history of Israel, and *thus* of the Church, and *thus* of the world, is included.

(4) There is a fourth stage of history; that since Christ the end has come into sight. This new beginning exists in the fact that the nations may now see and experience what Israel has been allowed to see and experience in the covenant with God. *The manifestation of the great acts*

of God to the nations determines the character of history after *Christ's death and resurrection.* This last sentence summarizes what we must now demonstrate and develop in this chapter.[1]

2. *The Great Turning-Point*[2]

The fact that there is no reference to a call to mission until after the resurrection of Christ has already drawn our attention several times. Let us now investigate this special relation between resurrection and mission in the world of nations.

A. It is a striking peculiarity that both the synoptic Gospels and the Gospel of John culminate in the pronouncement of the resurrection *and* the call to mission emerging from it. The clearest passage of all is found in Matt. 28: 18–20. We want, therefore, to follow up this pronouncement. The older explanations often began from the idea that this pericope contains a pronouncement of the ascension.[3] It is the great service of O. Michel that he has set forth convincingly that this passage had originally been connected with a completely different thought-world.[4]

"Our Matthew tradition regards Dan. 7: 13–14 as fulfilled and its triad simply as a Christological transformation of the Daniel passage. What Dan. 7: 13–14 has predicted has come to pass: 'The Son of Man came on the clouds of heaven, and was brought before the Ancient of Days, and to him was given dominion and glory and kingdom, that all peoples, nations, and languages should serve him.' *Thus the service of the nations is a portion of the enthronement of the Son of Man.* The ancient Oriental ceremony of the enthronement of a king comprises three events: exaltation, presentation (= declaration of exaltation) and enthronement (= transfer of dominion). This ceremony is transferred to Jesus in the thought-world of our text: the word of authority refers to the exaltation which has taken place, the command to mission

83

is nothing but the proclamation of the exaltation which has taken place, the secret of the Lordship of Jesus is hidden in the promise as well. From the homogeneity of these three sayings it could certainly be concluded that they have existed from the beginning as a unity. Probably our Evangelist has also combined resurrection, exaltation and installation into a unity, and has thus tinged Easter with the colours of the Second Coming of Jesus.

"Now it is also understandable why our Evangelist brings us no explicit story of the ascension, and why he alternatively does not let our text end with an ascension. *The decisive removal to the Father has taken place and is connected with the enthronement.* In the meantime the eternal Lordship of Christ over heaven and earth has begun. He discloses Himself to His disciples as a hidden yet present Son of Man and Lord, and now He summons them to proclaim the Lordship among the nations which has now begun. *The proclamation of the Gospel is thus the proclamation of the Lordship of Christ among the nations.* Matthew means that since Easter the Gospel has taken on a new form, like its Lord Himself. Perhaps also the various prophecies, Matt. 16: 27, 26: 64, correspond to this exaltation and enthronement which have taken place with Easter. Here we have Christology similar to the one we meet in Phil. 2: 5–11: 'Therefore God has highly exalted him and bestowed on him the name which is above every name, that at the name of Jesus every knee should bow, in heaven and on earth and under the earth, and every tongue confess that Jesus Christ is Lord, to the glory of God the Father.'

"The installation of Jesus into His Lordship and the proclamation necessarily resulting from it is thus eschatology which is fulfilled, which has become history. With Easter a new age has begun, the enthronement of a new ruler of the world, and the proclamation of this new ruler among the nations. *Mission is the summons of the Lordship of Christ.* The distinctive thing about this Christology is that, in the Easter event, the resurrection of the body is not being set forth so much as the elevation of the Lord into the new Messianic situation."

The significance of this statement is emphasized by the fact that the word "all" occurs four times: "all" authority, "all" nations, "all" that I have commanded, always (Greek: "all the days").[5] This indicates that, according to the judgment of the writer of the gospel himself, we are involved in an extremely important and all-embracing declaration. The resurrected and exalted Lord Himself gives to the joyous message a new form which must be brought to the nations.[6]

All authority has been given to me. The expressed premise of "me" prevents us from simply assuming "all authority" to mean a high position. It is not the *fact* of authority itself which is important, but the bearer of authority. The gospel is precisely that He who has been suffering, been crucified, died, been buried, and risen, has now gained all authority as a *gift* of the Father. In this way the whole world, visible and invisible (heaven and earth), has been wrested from the grip of any other powers whatsoever. The authority which rules heaven and earth is henceforth the authority of the abased and exalted Servant of God.

Go therefore and make disciples of all nations. This new, unheard-of reality is not to be made known to Israel alone, but must be passed on to "all nations". This expression forms a contrast to the Jews, Israel, to whom there is such frequent reference in this very Gospel of Matthew. (Cf. Matt. 1: 1–17, 2: 2, 10: 5–6, 15: 21–28, etc.) In this "go to all nations" there lies therefore the distinctive turning-point, the great change of direction of the gospel, indicated and prepared by earlier declarations of Jesus (e.g. Matt. 13: 38, 22: 1–14, 24: 14, etc.), but now coming into effect.

Mission was formerly based a little too one-sidedly and (even) almost exclusively on this "great commission". But the fault lay not in the fact that mission was based on *this* declaration, but in the fact that Matt. 28: 18–20 was isolated from the whole of the Biblical witness. For it cannot be denied that here, *and here for the first time*, the commission is given to go out among the nations.[7]

Here the limits to the preaching of the gospel which the apostles had been set before Jesus' resurrection (cf. Matt. 10: 5 ff.) are removed; all the world is to hear about the great salvation. This, however, can be achieved only by going forth, by visiting the nations. This going forth is linked to the task of making disciples as a guiding and determining *participium*. The fact that this *participium* is put first (going forth or after having gone forth, *participium aoristi*) places the emphasis on going, on travelling.

One will have to pass Israel's boundaries consciously and intentionally to be able to fulfil the order. In this "going forth" the world apostleship of the Christian Church is clearly indicated; the making of disciples can happen only in a movement of the disciples of Christ towards all nations.

Seen in the light of Christ's position of authority over all things (in heaven and on earth) a positive attitude towards "all nations" has come into being that overshadows anything negative that may have been said about the nations. This positive relationship has been given character and meaning by the order "make them into disciples of mine".[8]

All that I have commanded you. The *total* dominion over the *total* world of men must also come to expression in a *total* dedication and submission to what Jesus had commanded. That is not to say that life is to be submitted to a new impersonal *law* or legalism; it seems of great significance to me that there is no reference here to the "commandments of Jesus", but of "what I have commanded". The obedience is determined by the relation to Jesus Christ Himself, not by a conformity to an impersonal commandment.[9, 10]

There is nothing new in this teaching,[11] it is simply a matter of recollecting what Jesus has already said; it is therefore not a matter of a "secret teaching" or of a new law. In this respect what Jesus has commanded is reminiscent of what had had validity even "in the beginning" (cf. 1 John 2: 7). But it receives new authority because it is now *commanded* by Him who has received all authority. This "commanding" is a reference to the royal and divine glory which is spoken of in verse 18.[12]

Whereas "all nations" indicates the extensive area of authority of the exalted Lord, "all that I have commanded you" contains a reference to the intensive range of authority: *all* life and the whole man is claimed by Christ.[13]

I am with you always. After the proclamation and the commandment, the promise now follows. The presence of Christ is *the* great gift to His disciples. The promise of the presence is the fulfilment—but now for all nations—of the promise expressed in the name Yahweh (Exod. 3). In other words, the God of Israel has now made His presence in Israel into a presence among all nations at all times, till the day of consummation.

This reference to the consummation is not so much an indication that the call to mission will keep its authority until the consummation of the world (though I believe one might deduce this), as it is an indication of the *character of the presence of Jesus Christ:* it is a presence which is directed to the "consummation of the world". Proclamation, commandment to preach and make disciples, are carried and sent along not only by the promise of Christ's own presence but also by His own glance toward the consummation of the world. Therefore the attributes of discipleship are not only obedience to His command to proclamation, baptism and instruction to all nations, but *also* orientation to the consummation of the world as the last and deepest goal of Christ's work.

Here, then, is an implicit answer as to why, given Christ's resurrection, the Kingdom of God has not yet come, nor the complete end of all things. Christ's gaze is certainly directed toward this consummation (cf. Acts 1: 6–8), but this consummation is preceded by the preaching

87

of the gospel. On the other hand, this commission itself belongs to the signs and the consequences of this consummation (for Matt. 28: 18 speaks of the eschatological royal lordship of Christ).[14]

The convincing power of the proclamation of the gospel in the world is laid in the firm certainty of Christ's presence as a presence directed toward the consummation of the world. The promise of Christ's presence *always* gives rest and confidence anew each day, at every time, and under *all* circumstances, to do the work which He has commanded.[15]

From this short summary of the rich contents of the "great commission", its mighty significance and its abiding actuality are already apparent.

In the other Gospels the accent of the resurrection and mission accounts is different. In Mark 16: 14–20, the concern is for the world of men ("the whole creation" is here the world of men). This account thus misses the dimension of Matthew (*heaven* and earth), and in any case the differentiation of the latter. On the other hand, Mark accentuates more the intensive, comprehensive authority of Jesus (as superior power over unbelief, powers, sickness). In Luke 24: 44–53, the emphasis lies on the surprising element in God's activity, which makes victories out of defeats, changes sadness into joy, liberates us from sin and guilt, and enables us to sing praises. In the synoptics there is thus a difference of accent between *royal* authority, *liberating* authority, *forgiving* authority (Matt., Mark, Luke respectively).

John also takes his own place in comparison with the other Gospels; in 20: 21–23, he indicates the continuity of the sending of Jesus Christ by the Father and the sending of the disciples by Jesus; man is, as it were, the arm of God by which He directs His saving acts, man is taken up actively in God's design of salvation.[16]

From all the accounts, it is clear that the resurrection, as the crowning of Christ's work, is *the* first and great presupposition and condition for the proclamation of the gospel among the nations. The second is the gift of the Holy Spirit, with which we must now deal.[17]

B. The enduring presence of Christ which was promised in Matt. 28: 20, will be a presence in and through the Holy Spirit. If the resurrection of Christ is called a return, a parousia, then one could say this with as much, or even more justification, of the outpouring of the Holy Spirit. John, in particular, refers to the coming of the Holy Spirit as a return: John 14: 1–6, 15–19, 25–28, 15: 26, 16: 22; and Paul, too, in a very compact declaration: "now the Lord is the Spirit", 2 Cor. 3: 17.

This enduring presence of Christ in and through the Holy Spirit is to enable the disciples now in their turn to carry out the commission to preach the gospel to all nations. Emphasis is rightly laid by all sorts of publications on the fact that Christ Himself does His work of proclamation of the gospel through the Holy Spirit. He *charges* them to mission, certainly, but He does not *delegate* it to them. It is solely by the authority of the Holy Spirit that the disciples will be in a position to be witnesses of Christ to the uttermost parts of the earth, Acts 1: 6–8 (cf. Luke 24: 47 and John 20: 21). The Church's work of mission is bound both to Easter and to Pentecost. The Easter message can be brought to the nations only by the reality of Pentecost.[18] The Holy Spirit first makes man an instrument of God, His "arm" (cf. Isa. 8: 11, Ezek. 1: 3, etc.). He is the life-giving breath of God (Ezek. 37: 9, Heb. 11: 3).[19]

"The powers of the coming age" become visible in the power of the Holy Spirit. Therefore the Holy Spirit is both a fulfilment of the promise and the promise of fulfilment: He is the guarantee that the new world of God has already begun, as well as a sign that this new world is still to come.

The close connection between call to mission and Holy Spirit cannot be exaggerated. If the disciples, in Acts 1: 6–8, ask about the "restoration of the kingdom to Israel", they receive the answer: "you shall receive the power of the Holy Spirit *and* you shall be my witnesses". This "and" (*kai*) here has the same consecutive power as the "then" (*oun*) in Matt. 28: 19, and one might almost translate: you shall receive the power of the Holy Spirit *in order to* be my witnesses.

[The signs, too, under which the Holy Spirit was poured out, Acts 2: 1–11, are not insignificant for the course of the Gospel in the world: the Holy Spirit shall make His way with irresistible and life-giving power (the rush of wind, cf. Ezek. 37: 9); He shall conquer resistance and make the Church into living and powerful witnesses of His presence (the tongues of fire, cf. Exod. 3: 2, Matt. 3: 11); He shall make Himself intelligible in the world, and so establish unity and fellowship (the speaking in tongues, cf. Gen. 11).

The Holy Spirit guarantees the power of life in the Church, the presence of God in the world, and the publicizing of the Gospel. Nothing is left to men, not even to the apostles; *that*, however, is why everything *can* be delegated to the Church, and the Holy Spirit and the apostles can be drawn as close together as possible (see e.g. John 15: 26, Acts 5: 32, 15: 28)[20] as a "symbiosis". The Holy Spirit is the living promise and also the true presence of God (in Christ) in the world. So He is the first-fruits (Rom. 8: 23) and guarantee (2 Cor. 1: 22) of the future.]

C. By the resurrection of Christ and the gift of the Holy Spirit the way has now been freely given to the world of nations. But the gospel does not enter the world along capricious, arbitrary paths but in accordance with an unchanging pattern: Jerusalem—Israel—the Gentiles. Acts 1: 8 says this in clear words (this passage still names the Samaritans, too, as the portion of the world of Gentiles which is present, as it were, in the land of Israel itself). In spite of Israel's rejection of Jesus Christ (Acts 2: 36), Israel has not been rejected; she has complete precedence as regards the proclamation of the gospel. This precedence is still understood initially by many (by Peter himself, among others) as exclusiveness (Acts 10: 1–48, 11: 2, 3, 18),[21] and it is only in Antioch that the Christian Church loses altogether her character of a Jewish revival congregation (Acts 11: 20, 21, 26). Paul also goes to the Jews first before going to the Gentiles (Acts 13: 5, 14: 1, etc.) The Jews have first priority from a *heilesgeschichtlich* point of view, Rom. 3: 1 ff., but the Gentiles ("Greek" often represents the world of Gentiles) now follow as fellow-partners (cf. Rom. 1: 16, Eph. 3: 6).

The "progressive reduction" which the Old Testament image of history showed forth, mankind—Israel—the remnant of Israel—the One Servant of the Lord, now becomes a "progressive expansion": the One Messiah—the apostles as the nucleus and beginning of the new Israel and the Messianic congregation—Israel—the Gentiles=mankind.[22]

The whole structure of the Acts of the Apostles is determined by this course of the Gospel through the world, from the centre of Israel to the centre of the world, from Jerusalem to Rome.

Jerusalem *remains* the centre of Israel too, but with this difference, that the point of departure is no longer the Temple but rather the congregation at Jerusalem. In Jerusalem the disciples wait for the outpouring of the Holy Spirit, and the decisions for the whole Church are made out of Jerusalem (Acts 11: 22, 15: 1–22). The sending of Paul and Barnabas to the Gentiles may have taken place out of Antioch, but it was prepared by a decision of the Jerusalem congregation (cf. Acts 13: 2–3 with 11: 22, see also Gal. 2: 1–2).[23] Under the influence of the preaching among the Gentiles, however, we find the new outlines of another course of thought, which substitutes for the earthly Jerusalem a heavenly one (Gal. 4: 25–26, cf. Rev. 21: 10). In this regard, too, there is continuity in *Heilsgeschichte*, and at the same time a progression and a corresponding "new" addition in the revelation of salvation.[24] This fact is also clearly reflected in the prediction regarding the destruction of Jerusalem (Luke 13: 34, 19: 41–44, 21: 20–24, 23: 28–31 and parallels).

Jesus Christ Himself takes over the place of Jerusalem.[25] He is the central point around whom the nations will gather. To this they must be summoned and invited.

It is not the fact that one belongs to Israel, but one's belief in Jesus Christ as Him who was sent by God that is of decisive importance. An appeal to Abraham has no value unless one shares Abraham's faith and his works (Matt. 3: 9, John 8: 33–40).

This does not mean that the great significance of Israel as God's people is denied, but it means that from now on only those who belong to Christ are Israel in the sense of the history of salvation. The continuity of the history of salvation does not get lost, but the line is bent. This puts the controversy between a centripetal and a centrifugal movement, mentioned in the preceding chapters, in a new light; it is as it were put in its proper perspective by the much more important question—what think ye of Christ?[26]

Yet it is this very question that forces us to consider the question as to whether *the community of Christ* should be looked upon as the continuation of Israel or as an entirely new entity? Are the nations being *gathered up* unto the new Israel, or are the children of the Kingdom being scattered over the world like seed in order that they shall call all nations into the Kingdom? (Cf. Matt. 13: 28.)[27]

In the synoptic Gospels the idea of the new Israel, in and through Christ the salt of the earth and the light of the world, clearly predominates, even though the synoptics themselves hold different opinions and have different aims. In the Gospel according to St. John, however, the term "Jews" as used there clearly indicates strangeness and even hostility towards Jesus. It is significant, however, that in their negative attitude, too, it is the Jews who represent "the world". Paul's Epistles are based on several different lines of thought. Some say that he follows two lines of thought.[28]

The congregation of Christ is to be understood first of all as the true Israel. The old nation is Israel at the level of the *old* dispensation; the new nation is also Israel, at the level of the new dispensation. Christians who were Jews are the "remnants of Israel", and only by unity with this remnant do the Gentile Christians also belong to Israel. So it would appear that for Paul there are two points of view: (1) the Christians, not the Jews, are the congregation of God, because the important thing is not Israel according to the flesh, but Israel according to the Spirit (so strong, e.g. in Galatians); (2) there is only one people of God, namely Israel, and the Gentile Christians are taken into this one people as proselytes (so especially, e.g. in Romans).

The first accentuates the new creation which has begun in and through Christ, the second the *heilsgeschichtlich* continuity. The first indicates the severity and the freedom of God, the second the faithfulness to His promises. But the most important thing is that over against Jews and Gentiles something new has come, the third race (1 Cor. 10: 32) that is particularly characterized by the fact that it is the body of Christ and the temple of the Holy Spirit. Therefore the opposition between Jews and Gentiles has lost its particular significance both inside and outside the Church. The Church, as the new people of God, has taken over the place of Israel and the (hidden) centre of history and of the world, and this new people is still only the beginning of both the new manhood and the whole new creation (2 Cor. 5: 17, Gal. 6: 15, 1 Cor. 15: 28).

In Paul's apostleship the continuity of God's work in and for Israel, as well as the newness of the new era, become apparent in an unusual way. One can only obtain the right insight into the complicated relationship between Israel, the community of Christ and the world of nations if one considers this apostleship in its own and quite unique significance.

3. Paul's Apostleship[29]

If we want to understand the significance of Paul as the apostle of the heathen we depend on two sources, namely the Acts of the Apostles and Paul's own epistles. This is not the place to go deeply into the structure and construction of that magnificent book by the architect among the Evangelists, St. Luke, whose Acts is as beautifully composed as his Gospel is. We shall only underline that which is of importance to our subject.

A. The route of the Gospel is the road from Jerusalem, the centre of Israel, to Rome, the centre of the world. This journey, however much a matter of course it may seem to us, is so strange and unprecedented that it can only be explained by repeatedly pointing to the intervention of God Himself.

Preaching the gospel to Samaria is already a transgression of the boundaries of Israel, pointing to the nature of the gospel, which crosses all boundaries (cf. Acts 1:8), but it still takes place within reach of Israel's old country boundaries (Acts 8:4-25). The baptism of the Ethiopian, who came from the end of the earth to adore Israel's God, still lies within Israel's spiritual horizon (Acts 8:26-40). Peter's being sent to the heathen Cornelius, who admittedly lives within the confines of Israel but apparently does not live within the horizon of the greatest of the apostles, announces the great turning point. It is pointed out to us emphatically and repeatedly (which is characteristic of the book of Acts) that God Himself intervenes. He indicates to Peter that a new era has begun, in which the distinction between Jew and heathen vanishes as far as the preaching of the gospel is concerned. In our opinion it is no coincidence that Luke places this occurrence, related in Acts 10-11:17, after Saul's conversion. He, too, has been called direct from heaven, through a particular revelation of Christ "for he is a chosen vessel unto me, to bear my name before the Gentiles, and kings, and the children of Israel" (Acts 9: 15). When Saul has been called to be God's tool, Peter (and through him the community at Jerusalem) is warned to accept this turning towards the world of the heathen that God wants. This explains two things: (i) the particular charismatic nature of the apostleship to the heathen, which is of an almost violent character—Paul becomes an apostle after he, who strongly opposed Christ, has been arrested by Him on the road to Damascus; (ii) it is the community itself that actually supports this apostleship to the heathen, for they are convinced by divine intervention (Peter's vision) and by Peter's authority: thus God granted also to the Gentiles the repentance unto life (Acts 11: 18).

When the Jewish Christians from Cyprus and Cyrene also preach the gospel to the Greeks (which in this case is practically synonymous with *goyyim, ethne,* heathen) the hand of the Lord is with them and a great number are converted. In view of this rush of heathen Barnabas is sent from Jerusalem (!) to Antioch and Barnabas in his turn requisitions Saul of Tarsus. They work in Antioch for a full year and are then sent to Jerusalem with gifts of love donated by the community (Jews and Gentile Christians), they return and are then, by a special indication of the Holy Spirit, separated and sent forth; that is when the missionary work among the nations actually starts (Acts 13: 1–5). It is clear that Paul was not *exclusively* the preacher of the gospel among the Gentiles. The reference in Gal. 2: 9 to the arrangement between the apostles in Jerusalem on the one hand and Paul and Barnabas on the other, that the former were to work among the Jews and the latter among the Gentiles, is to be understood geographically, not ethnographically and not exclusively.[30] This tallies with the fact that from the very beginning Paul and Barnabas preached the gospel first to the Jews (Acts 13: 5, cf. 9: 15) and only afterwards go to the Gentiles. It seems to me that this fact should not be overestimated in a theological sense; Paul goes to the synagogue not only because

Israel has a priority in the history of salvation, but also because there, among the proselytes, he finds points of contact for the preaching of the gospel among the Gentiles.[31]

The conclusion that Paul's apostleship among the Gentiles has a pronounced *geographical* component is obvious; he is not the only apostle of the Gentiles but he is the most prominent one. That is why he can be contrasted with the twelve apostles; he does in the world of nations what they do among the Jews in their own country—he is the great world-witness for Jesus Christ.

Much has been written about Paul's apostleship as compared with that of the twelve apostles. It cannot be denied that it is characterized by a (certain amount of) *excentricity*.[32] Antioch (be it with the sanction of Jerusalem—Acts 11: 22) becomes a second centre, beside Jerusalem. The term "Christians" originated in Antioch, for it was there that it became clear—through the large number of Gentile Christians in the community—for the first time that those who believed in Christ constituted a third group beside Jews and Gentiles (Acts 11: 26). Paul is sent forth from Antioch. He himself always saw his own apostleship as something unique, he refers to himself as to someone born untimely, who is not worthy to bear the name of apostle (1 Cor. 15: 8).[33] In other words, his apostleship is something out of the usual, but not therefore less valid. It is well known that in almost all his epistles he places great emphasis on his lawful apostleship, given to him by God Himself.[34] His unusual calling to the apostleship accentuates its uniqueness and he is strongly aware of being an apostle of the Gentiles.[35]

B. It cannot be said often enough that Paul's apostleship is not only based on an abnormal calling but also has an abnormal *nature* and abnormal *contents;* in the first place to Paul as a Jew, but also to *all* Jews, for they partly "expected Israel's consolation" and knew of "a light for the Gentiles", but they could not but experience the "mission among the Gentiles" as something unprecedented and unknown. Was it not Jesus Himself who had admonished the disciples to address themselves to the lost sheep of the house of Israel only?

Surprise and amazement about the fact that the Gentiles, too, are "fellow heirs, members of the same body and partakers of the promise in Christ Jesus" (Eph. 3: 6) can clearly be heard in Eph. 2: 11–3: 21, one of the most important testimonies regarding Paul's apostleship among the Gentiles. It is made clear here, if anywhere, that the mission among the Gentiles cannot possibly be seen as a continuation of the Judaic making of proselytes during the diaspora.[36] Then it was only a matter of a few individuals from the world of nations and for them there would always have been room in Israel, geographically as well as spiritually. If Paul had been only the Jewish-Christian inheritor of a Judaic missionary tradition, there would have been no cause for him to speak so emotionally and ecstatically about his calling as an apostle of the Gentiles. The proselytic mission originated in the conviction of the unique nature of Israel as the people of God, the elect nation. Paul's apostleship became possible when the wall that separated Israel and the nations fell. In Christ the fullness of the times began (Eph. 1: 10, 11) and that means the unity of everything, in heaven and earth, under His dominion. No contrast, no break, no alienation can go on existing and remain valid. They who used to be "alienated from the commonwealth of Israel and strangers to the covenants of promise, having no hope and without God in the world" (Eph. 2: 12) are now made nigh by the blood of Christ (Eph. 2: 13). The wall between Israel and the Gentiles, a wall that also means hostility, was demolished by Christ. He is peace (*shalom, eirene*) and now there is no longer any difference; the former strangers and aliens are now fellow-citizens with the saints and are of the household of God (Eph. 2: 19). A new temple arises, not an Israelitic temple but an oecumenical one (Eph. 2: 21, 22), an habitation of God through the Spirit.

It is difficult for us now to realize how revolutionary these things must have sounded to Israelitic and non-Israelitic ears. Paul deduced this unprecedented turn in history from promises in the Old Testament (cf., e.g. Rom. 15: 9–13, 10: 4–21), but that did not lessen the surprise and joy, because their fulfilment far surpasses all ideas, expectations and promises. It is the "justification of the godless", the justification by faith, that opened the road to the nations (Rom. 3: 27–29). Israel looked for it in vain in the works of the law. Abraham already lived from his faith and thus became the prototype of the believers among the Gentiles (Rom. 4: 11), a father of many nations (Rom. 4: 18) and heir of the world (Rom. 4: 13). The Scriptures foresaw that God justifies the heathen through faith (Gal. 3: 8) and preaches before the gospel unto Abraham—In thee shall all nations be blessed. That is why everyone, Jew or Greek, slave or freeman, male or female, can be a child of God by faith in Christ Jesus (Gal. 3: 26–28).

We cannot get away from the conclusion that from now on only he who belongs to Christ can be of the seed of Abraham, i.e. member of the people of God; "And if ye be Christ's, then are ye Abraham's seed, and heirs according to the promise" (Gal. 3: 29).

In a theological sense Paul did here what to Jewish ears was incredible; the line of descent runs from Abraham via Christ to the world of the Gentiles and Abraham himself has become the prototype of the Gentile Christian! This was an *Umwertung aller Werte* (revaluation of all values), a setting aside of Israel according to the flesh, a relocation of the centre of God's acts from Israel to the world of the Gentiles; that which used to be ex-centric turns out to be central in God's design for salvation.

Paul now knows himself to be the herald of this new reality in Christ. In Eph. 3: 1–13, he refers to the preaching entrusted to him by the grace of God; the mystery of Christ that used to be unknown has been made known to him by a revelation and he, in his turn, is allowed to make known to the people this mystery as the gospel, as a message of joy. This preaching of the mystery ("economy of the mystery") does not only pass across the boundaries of Israel and the world of the Gentiles but even across the boundaries of the world of men; the principalities and powers in heavenly places are informed by the community (=the oecumenical community, consisting of Jews and non-Jews) of the manifold wisdom of God (Eph. 3: 10).

The exalted words that Paul uses when he talks about the grace that fell to his share, of preaching to the Gentiles the inscrutable riches of Christ, show clearly how strange, how surprising and how full of mystery the preaching of the gospel to the Gentiles is (cf. also Col. 1: 26–27). The strangeness, the abnormal nature of Paul's calling to the apostleship correspond to the strangeness, the abnormal nature of his preaching as preaching *among the Gentiles*. In his letter to the Ephesians, Paul rises to an almost ecstatic culmination in the affirmation that from now on a man, whether Jew or Gentile, can "be filled with all the fullness of God" only as a fellow-saint, in community with all others (Eph. 3: 18). There is one community, one body, one Spirit, one Lord, one faith, one baptism, one God and Father of all (Eph. 4: 3–6). And it is only from this unity that the variety of gifts and services can be made to serve the "fulness of Christ" (Eph. 4: 7–16).

In this letter to the Ephesians we are confronted with an exalted and profound credo concerning Christ as the turning point in history, the break-through of the new world. As the riches and wisdom of God He is at one and the same time the mystery and the power of the new creation. It is the *community of the world of nations* which makes Him known as the manifold wisdom of God to the heavenly powers.

Paul writes to the Romans that as Jesus Christ's minister to the Gentiles he has to bring an offering from the Gentiles that is acceptable in the eyes of God (Rom. 15:

99

16). This consists in effecting obedience to the faith (Rom. 16: 26) *among all nations*, thus making Paul's apostleship, even more than that of the twelve apostles, a sign of the *fulfilment of the times*, of God's eschatological acting.

C. This shows the ex-centricity of Paul's apostleship, but also the ex-centricity of God's acting in Jesus Christ; the former centre, Israel, has lost its significance as a centre. The Gentiles now take its place, or rather the community consisting of Jews and Gentiles does. Paul's well-known explanation in Rom. 9–11, in which he stresses the strangeness, the ex-centricity of his preaching to the Gentiles, which is at the same time a sign and a warning of the end, shows how hard it was even for him to understand this ex-centricity of God's acting.

Eph. 2-3 looks upon the community formed from the world of nations as the fruit of the revelation of the mystery that Gentiles will also be fellow-heirs of the promise in Christ Jesus, while Rom. 9–11 affirms that these riches of the Gentiles arise from Israel's fall and failure (Rom. 11: 11–12).

One should not conclude from the fact that the Gentiles have been accepted that Israel has been rejected. Paul himself with the remnant according to the election (Rom. 11: 1–6) is the proof that God has not rejected His people. That which is happening in the world of the Gentiles is directed towards the salvation of Israel itself; just as Israel has not received its place in the history of salvation because of itself but because of the Gentiles, so the community formed out of the Gentiles has not received its place in the history of salvation because of itself, but because of Israel in order to arouse it to jealousy.[37] There is an interdependence between the salvation of the Gentiles and that of Israel; they cannot and may not be detached from each other.[38] Just as the fall of Israel opened the road to the "fullness of the Gentiles", so this fullness of the Gentiles will, in its turn, lead to the fullness, the acceptance, the salvation of Israel (Rom. 11: 12, 25, 26). This is a divine mystery which cannot be fathomed or gauged; one can only stammer about it in amazement (Rom. 11: 34–36).

It is clear from Rom. 9–11 that to Paul the reconciliation of the world (Rom. 11: 15), of which the preaching of the gospel among the Gentiles is the sign and prelude (Rom. 10: 16–18), is at the same time a *penultimate reality*. The mission to the Gentiles, of which Paul is the characteristic and principal representative, cannot be appreciated except as *the* great happening "between the times"; the coming of Jesus Christ in the flesh and His return at the end. God has already revealed His last plans and carried them out in Christ. All that is left now is for the revelation of the mystery to be completed and finished.

The closed world of nations that God has allowed to walk in their own ways is now confronted with the great salvation which calls upon all people everywhere to repent (Acts 14: 16, 17: 30).

If we compare what has been said so far in this section, it appears that according to Eph. 2–4, as well as to Rom. 9–11, the preaching of the gospel among the Gentiles is a strange, unexpected, surprising occurrence. In Eph. 2–4, the emphasis is on the execution of a divine plan of salvation for the world; in Rom. 9–11, it is on the temporary nature of the coming of the Gentiles that will find its end in the salvation of the whole of Israel. We shall have to accept these two ideas without wanting to make them into one whole that fits. In Paul's own person the centripetal and centrifugal aspects of the preaching are brought together. It is he, as the apostle of the Gentiles, who passes all boundaries to be Christ's minister everywhere in the world, who calls upon the Gentiles to bring offerings that find favour in God's eyes (Rom. 15: 16), it is he, as the son of Israel, who even when he is preaching among the Gentiles is still gathering Israel, taking the nations home and arousing the jealousy of his flesh and blood (Rom. 11: 1, 13, 14).

D. When Christ is the centre of the preaching and belief in Him is of decisive importance, the community which is gathered around Him becomes itself a "preacher of the joyful message". Even though the apostles, and particularly Paul, are the first to spread the gospel, they are not the only ones to do so. Even the term "apostle" is flexible and is not restricted to Paul and the twelve (cf. e.g. Rom. 16: 7). The community in Thessalonica became an example to all believers in Macedonia and Achaia (1 Thess. 1: 7, 8). During his imprisonment Paul's task is taken over by others (Phil. 1: 14). It is part of a Christian's armour to be "shod with the equipment of the gospel of peace" (Eph. 6: 15).[39]

The community of Christ also takes over Israel's task in that the mission from Israel to the Gentiles now becomes the mission from the Gentiles (Christians) to Jews and Gentiles (heathen). The progress of the gospel in the world of Paul's time was made possible not only by his apostleship but also by this activity of the community. It is remarkable that so little is said in the New Testament about the obligation, the task of preaching the gospel. Apparently it was so obvious that the glad tidings were to be passed on, that it was hardly necessary to remind anyone of it. It does appear, though, that some were *particularly* charged with the preaching among the Gentiles. One is involuntarily reminded of the evangelists (Eph. 4: 11) and the prophets (1 Cor. 12: 28). One rarely finds an admonition to preach the gospel in Paul's epistles. What he does ask for is intercession in order that the word of the Lord may speed on (2 Thess. 3: 1).

In the haste which becomes apparent from these words, Paul professes his belief and expresses the hope that Jesus Christ will come soon. His preaching is characterized by the glow and tenseness of expectation.[40] This also determines the aim of his preaching. When in his letters he stresses time and again that one should live as a follower of God (Eph. 5: 1), of Christ (Eph. 5: 2, Phil. 2: 3–11), of himself as an apostle (1 Cor. 4: 16, 11: 1, Phil. 3: 17,

1 Thess. 1: 6, 2: 14), he does so because of the Second Coming of Christ, the coming of the Kingdom (Eph. 5: 5, 1 Thess. 5: 23, 2 Cor. 11: 2). The contents and aim of his preaching can be summarized as follows: Jesus Christ is Lord, Lord of the community and therefore of the world, the Lord who has come and will come, who must be known, expected and honoured among all nations. That is why he, Paul, wants to preach the gospel in each and every province of the Roman Empire, and particularly in every large town, and as far as "the ends of the earth" (Spain), in order that the name of Christ shall be mentioned everywhere (Rom. 15: 22–24, cf. 15: 19–20).

The eschatological connection of the Pauline mission must be taken into account. The activity of the apostles is a fragment of the history of the end. Rapidly the fashion of this world passes away, and at the time St. Paul writes the letter to the Romans, the daybreak of the new era is already nearer than when he came unto belief. The generation to which he and his readers belong is the one during which the aeons coincide. For what has happened in Christ and what goes on with the Church, is the breakthrough of the future. That is why one must speed up: salvation must be preached to all nations, carried forward to the ends of the earth, before the end comes. Here is the reason for the bold plan of a mission to Spain, which is for ancient ideas even the utmost part of the earth. The event to which the mission belongs is therefore not a transitory period but it is to serve immediately the realization of God's world-purpose; it binds one to full commitment and calls for a decision for eternity. Where this calling is obeyed, there is anticipated and realized a fragment of God's eternal world.[41]

CHAPTER 7

TOWARDS A THEOLOGY OF MISSION?

1. Mission and World History[1]

IF WE ARE TO DO JUSTICE TO THE BIBLICAL DATA regarding mission, and thereby take account of the opinions of many theological directions and convictions, it is healthy to remember the wise word of O. Michel:

> All genuine theology is in battle against theologizing, abstracting, theorizing, and against the attempt to replace the genuine Biblical and historical motive by a philosophical transformation. Genuine theology is acquainted with insoluble tensions and self-defining thought-forms of the holy Scriptures, which cannot become a part of any human scheme nor of any theological system. At present we are in love with simplifications, while the Bible glorifies humble simplicity; at present we wish easy solutions, while the Bible strengthens us with solutions for travelling; at present we wish again and again to hear ourselves, while the Bible would invite us to the hearing of the naked word.[2]

Now if we attempt to set forth the present state of discussion regarding the place of mission in world history, we must take special account of the "insoluble tensions" to which the foregoing quotation refers.

A. In the first place, the Holy Scriptures make clear to us that the proclamation of the gospel among the nations is possible only

   (i) By the voluntary sacrifice of Jesus Christ on the cross, which is both a sign of God's pity *and* of Israel's obstinacy;

  (ii) By the resurrection of Christ from the dead, through which He has received the dominion of the world;

(iii) Through the gift of the Holy Spirit, which enables the apostles and the community to witness.

One might say that by this means a new period in world history has dawned and a new creation has arisen around Christ. Christ is the end of the Old Testament and the First-born of the new creation, the end of a world, the beginning of a new one, "the hinge of history".[3] Mission, seen under this aspect of the new world, is not only a *consequence* of Christ's dominion of the world, but it is also the *actualization* of it. The proclamation of the gospel is the *form* of the Kingdom of God. Acts 1: 6–8 must surely be viewed in this light: the expected establishment of the Kingdom for Israel will take place at a point of time determined by God, but the manifestation of the Kingdom is an affair of the witness of men by the power of the Holy Spirit. In the Holy Spirit it is Christ Himself who witnesses, but at the same time it is the disciples who witness. Strange things are being said to us about this unity-in-tension of divine and human witness, over and over again in the New Testament.

[Compare, for example, Acts 15: 28: "For it has seemed good to the Holy Spirit and to us," with Rom. 8: 16: "It is the Spirit himself bearing witness *with* our spirit." In the first passage the Holy Spirit leads and men follow; in the second the witness of the Holy Spirit is an accompaniment of human witness!]

In the light of this new beginning the proclamation of the gospel among the nations must be understood as the actualization of the eschatological prospects. The new world already *is*, but it is so only for him who sees the actuality of Christ's dominion in the proclamation of the gospel in the world.

Here one might say (though in one sense it is too strongly put): the proclamation is not dependent on world history, but rather world history is dependent on proclamation, because and in so far as this is the manifestation of Christ's dominion over the world. But it is important not to accentuate the reality of Christ's dominion at the expense of the *tentativeness* and *hiddenness* of this dominion.

[In Roman Catholic and High Church thinking, the dominion of Christ and the Kingdom of God are understood as realized in the Church, so that the Church takes over the *place* of the Kingdom almost wholly. So *both* the hiddenness *and* the tentativeness of Christ's dominion are robbed of their reality and one loses sight of the fact that "the form of this world is passing away" (1 Cor. 7: 31). The same one-sidedness lies at the basis of the "social gospel" idea and of its offshoots, and in general of the idealistic, social-ethical narrowing of the Kingdom of God. "The New Testament knows no other progression in history than that the end is coming nearer. Therefore all ideas of a gradual actualization of the Kingdom of God in this world, or of a Christianization of the world, have been banished to the area of illusions."[4]]

B. In the publications of the last few decades (at least on the European continent), the proclamation of the gospel is seen much more as a sign of the end than as a sign of fulfilment. We have been greatly influenced in this regard by the observations of Oscar Cullmann. "The missionary proclamation of the Church, her preaching of the Gospel, gives to the time between resurrection and the Second Coming of Christ its *heilsgeschichtlich* meaning in connection with Christ's present dominion."[5] The evidence for this thesis lies in Mark 13: 10 and Matt. 24: 14, in which mission is named among divine signs along with woes such as wars, famine, etc. "It is not true that the coming of the Kingdom depends upon the *result* of this preaching; rather upon the *fact* of the preaching."[6]

By this view, mission too, like all "signs", allows not a single calculation nor any single limitation upon this or any other generation. According to this early Christian idea, the Church must proclaim the gospel to "the whole world in every generation".[7]

[The remark regarding calculation is obviously directed

against the apocalyptic narrowing of the Kingdom of God, as if one could force the end closer either by calculation or by great activity. Matt. 24: 14 does not speak of the "must" of proclamation but simply of the future actuality of proclamation. Future is different from imperative. Further, Acts 1: 8: "you *shall* be my disciples"—this is future, not imperative. Man is only a producing instrument and the *commandment* emerges only in the second place. Mark 13: 10, too ("must", followed by a passive), is an indication of a *heilsgeschichtlich* necessity rather than of a commandment laid upon man. This does not mean that the command is denied, but it certainly renders impossible every human convulsion and over-exertion of human activity.[8]]

Since about 1930 the eschatological character of mission has been receiving more and more emphasis. Some even explain the theological impasse of the I.M.C. conference at Willingen in 1952 by this tension between the character of mission as expectation and fulfilment, of Kingdom and Church.[9]

The resistance against this, especially from the Anglo-Saxon side,[10] and to a lesser degree from the Eastern Orthodox side,[11] is not yet free from misunderstandings. Church and mission are still often contrasted with each other as static and dynamic, introverted and extraverted, and the eschatological character of mission is still often confused with apocalyptic agitation and overhastiness. The blame for this should certainly not be placed on those who during the past few decennia have pleaded for this eschatological foundation—Hartenstein, Freytag, Hoekendijk, Manson, Warren and others.

Nevertheless, during the past few years the uncertainty as to whether missionary work is justified has been increasing. It is more and more widely recognized

(i) That from its beginning the Church of Christ as a whole has been of an eschatological nature. Since the resurrection of Christ and the descent of the

Holy Spirit, the Church and the world are both in the same eschatological circumstances in all their actions and responsibilities—the end of the ages has come (1 Cor. 10: 11);

(ii) That during the whole of its existence the Church of Christ is the servant of the world, sent forth into the world. The community exists for the world, because it is the community of Jesus Christ.

Its existence is not purpose in itself, however wonderful and glorious it may be as such, also in all that it comprises for its individual members. The illuminating power of the Holy Spirit draws, drives and pushes [the congregation] away from its existence as such, away also from all that its members receive, experience and go through; away also from all that has been promised to them personally. And only in following this guidance and impact, it is and becomes the true congregation of Jesus Christ.[12] The real congregation of Jesus Christ is the congregation which is, in and with its foundation, sent into the world by God. Just as such it is there for the world. Not because of value, authority and power, which is immanent in its nature as creature, as a nation among others, but because of a given power of attorney, given to her in and with its special foundation as *this* people and therefore as a genuine power.[13]

Now the question forcibly arises what is specific or unique in missionary work as *äussere Mission*, as "foreign mission(s)". Norman Goodall has formulated this question as follows:

What is the theological significance of "foreign" mission within the total responsibility of the Church? The more this total responsibility is emphasized the less easy it is to retain for the foreign obligation a unique element of call and separation. Have the ends of the earth a theological significance comparable with the end of time? In the vocational experience of countless missionaries (of varying races and from younger and older Churches) there appears to be a convincing testimony to this unique element in the call of foreign service. This being so, can it be articulated theologically in a manner which will illumine afresh its significance for the whole Church?[14]

In my opinion those who have advocated the eschatological foundation of missionary work with so much force should be given lasting credit for having drawn the conclusions from the academic theological discussion in favour of missionary work that were to be more generally recognized later on. Does this mean that they have understood the essence and the calling of the Church of Christ in the world better and sooner than others have?

What is the connection between this new vision of the Church as it appears, for instance, in the above words of Karl Barth, and in missionary work? And in what way has an answer been looked for and found to the question as to the nature and the intrinsic right of missionary work in the whole of the work of the community of Christ during the past few years?

2. *Current Questions*

In our attempt to understand the basis and motive of mission from the Bible, what we have thus far discovered can be summarized in a statement by Walter Freytag:

> Without mission, history is nothing but human history whose progress consists at best in the intensifying of its catastrophe. But if we know of the coming Kingdom, we cannot rejoice in the promise without proclaiming it. The Lord is near.[15]

But the word "mission", even in this quotation, must be detached from an all too narrow conception of it. We shall have to be aware of a double danger which Bishop Neill has pointed out: the word mission can be made *so* broad that it becomes almost meaningless: "If everything is mission, nothing is mission."[16] On the other hand, we dare not seek a "theology of missionary societies" as "a theological justification of what we have done in the past and of what we are trying to do in the present."[17]

We may formulate the questions, put in the previous paragraph, in this way:[18] Is there a relation between the eschatological and geographical character of the missionary's task? (Consider, for instance, the meanings of the expression "the ends of the earth".) In the light of these Biblical considerations are "foreign missions" a theological necessity or a historical contingency? If the former is true, does it include the obligation to preach the gospel in *foreign* lands?

It is these questions in particular which have been the occasion for writing the preceding chapters, and we shall deal with the topics in this order:

A. The connection between the eschatological and the geographical character of the task of the Church;

B. The character of foreign missions as a theological necessity and as a historical contingency;

C. The peculiar significance of the preaching of the gospel in foreign lands.

A. The question of the connection between the eschatological and the geographical character of the task of the Church has often been answered. Wilhelm Andersen represents general opinion when he remarks: "The missionary enterprise is an eschatological entity, in the sense of future eschatology as much as in that of realized eschatology. . . . The geographical and temporal components belong to the very essence of missionary service."[19]

Andersen bases this, as many have done before him, on the expressions "ends of the earth" and "end of days". I think it must be recognized that the expression "the last of days" occurs *much* more often in the Bible than "the last" or "the uttermost parts of the earth".

Furthermore, we noticed in Chapter 2 that the eschatological character of the Old Testament expressions "the end of days", or "in coming days", is not so strict as was once thought; they do refer to a decisive moment in the future, but they can also be used with another meaning.

In the New Testament, "the last days" can mean the days which have broken forth with Christ (Heb. 1: 1) and the Holy Spirit (Acts 2: 17), but also the time of the Last Judgment and the Second Coming (e.g. John 11: 24, 12: 48, 1 Pet. 1: 5). The accent in the New Testament, as we have seen, lies at least as much on Him who has come as upon that which was expected. The expression "ends of the earth" occurs in the New Testament only twice, in Acts 1: 8, and in Matt. 12: 42 (Luke has a parallel in 11: 31); but in the synoptic passage the word *eschata* is not used. The connection between "the end of days" and "the ends of the earth" is no doubt inspired mostly by Matt. 24: 14 and Mark 13: 10, though here the reference is to "the whole world". But this expression refers to the whole non-Israelitic world, like the expression "all nations". It occurs to me that we are to see in the expression "the ends of the earth", which occurs in connection with the call to mission only in Acts 1: 8, a synonym of "the whole world" and "all nations".

Therefore our first thought as we hear the expression must be that it is an indication of the intensive and extensive universality of salvation. This universality includes geographical comprehensiveness, but the latter is not emphasized. The emphasis in the New Testament is always on the "going", but this indicates a crossing of the boundary between Israel and the Gentiles rather than geographical boundaries, though the first naturally does not exclude the second. We are concerned here with emphases, but these may become very important, as is the case with the expression "uttermost parts of the earth". I think this is why the latter has received so much emphasis—because in missionary circles the phrase echoes the idea of "far-away places", particularly the lands of the "Orient". Missions were only missions if it was a matter of far countries, "overseas", particularly in Asia and Africa.

Now to be consistent with this line of thinking, the countries of Europe and America should be considered by the younger Churches in Asia and Africa as the "uttermost parts of the earth". I think, therefore, it is best to confine the term "ends of the earth" to its Biblical value (and not to conceive of it too strictly in geographical terms): the world, indeed the whole world to the very farthest corners. For Jesus' disciples, Europe belonged to the "uttermost parts of the earth", and at that time it did, too! And this "uttermost" reached no farther than the western coasts of the Mediterranean Sea.

Therefore, it seems to me illegitimate theologically to found mission as "foreign mission" on a correlation between the "end of days" and the "ends of the earth", unless the latter is purged of its non-Biblical "Western" significance. It is a boundary notion which indicates that Christ's dominion knows no geographical boundaries either. In other words, the missionary commission is from the very beginning an ecumenical commission, a commission which concerns the whole inhabited world. Thus the criterion is simply: that one must have *heard* of Christ in order to be able to believe in Him. Thus He must be preached everywhere, and to that end the messengers of the gospel must be sent (Rom. 10: 11–15).

We may therefore summarize by remarking: (1) that the Biblical eschatology certainly has a geographical component, to the extent that the whole world belongs to Christ and He must thus be preached to the whole world; (2) that the theology of mission makes valid use of these eschatological and geographical factors *only* when it has completely detached itself from schemes such as East-West, white-coloured, etc. The only distinction which is relevant "to the uttermost parts of the earth" is whether one has heard of Christ or not. If not, then there is a concern for mission, whether far off or near. In the Bible, "far off" and "near" are much more *heilsgeschichtlich* than geographical distinctions! (Eph. 2: 13), confined by the historical place of Israel and Jerusalem (Acts 1: 8).[20]

B. The next question is *how* are we really to think of

mission: as a theological necessity or as a historical contingency?

To begin with the latter alternative: the missionary work of the Western Churches during the last three centuries obviously cannot be considered apart from the historical constellation. So much has been written about this that we need not say a word about it here. But it is not right to speak of historical contingency. History is anything but contingent. "The whole idea of history takes its rise from Christian theology, from the gospel and its proclamation, from God's revelation in Israel and in Jesus Christ. Revelation has made existence historical."[21] For in the historical activity of mission by Western Christendom the God of history has had a hand, and the whole significance of the so-called Vasco da Gama period (from a *heilsgeschichtlich* point of view) could have lain in the fact that the name of Christ was declared among the many nations which had not known Him theretofore. One must not underrate the significance of this: the "oecumene" of the twentieth century is inconceivable without the missions of the eighteenth and nineteenth centuries. For this reason one can be both ashamed and surprised that only a very small proportion of the Christian Church in the West has shouldered the burden of missions. It is my conviction that the Church has been manifested more clearly in the much-defamed groups of "friends of mission" than in the "official Church", which at best accepted a benevolently neutral attitude toward mission (at least on the European continent—but was it really so much better in the Anglo-Saxon lands?).

The "colonial period" in world history has also been the period of the proclamation of the gospel, and although this proclamation has suffered under the "colonial infection", and has even degenerated here and there under it, nevertheless, the gospel is no longer to be thought of apart from the lands which were once colonized: the name of Christ has been named, His Church established, and the

Kingdom of God is at hand in the lands which were formerly "far off". That this could have happened in the midst of the aloofness of the greater portion of Christendom is one more indication that the proclamation of the gospel among the nations is not a human but a divine act, a work of the exalted Christ and His Spirit. Therefore "the West" has no reason to boast about what has arisen in "the East", but "East and West" shall both "sing of the ways of the Lord, for great is the glory of the Lord" (Ps. 138: 5).

Furthermore, it seems to me of the greatest possible significance, from the *heilsgeschichtlich* point of view, that the Church across the world is now learning anew to understand that Jesus Christ is the hope of the world, and *therefore* the meaning of history, the Alpha and the Omega. The proclamation of the gospel must therefore make progress even if the pattern of present-day mission work be completely forgotten. It is gradually becoming clear that the pattern which has been followed up to now (one-way traffic in missions, spiritual and financial dependence of the younger Churches, and the like) is old, obsolete, and thus about to disappear (cf. Whitby–Willingen–Ghana). The sooner we are ready to follow the God of history, the more clearly will He show us the image of future missionary activity of His *whole* people over the whole earth. It appears to me that when expressions are used such as "partnership in obedience" and "mission in unity", these coming relationships are still only very vaguely indicated. Did not Paul see *more* when he (Eph. 3: 18, 19) saw the *unity* of the Church in the joyful expectation of the fullness of God, which can be achieved only *together* with all the saints? The progress of the proclamation of the gospel over the *whole* world by the *whole* Church has this deep impulse: the love of Christ is so great, so wide, so long, so high, so deep, and it reaches so far above all knowledge, that it can be conceived only "together with all the saints". The all-embracing love of Christ demands a "comprehensive approach".

In summary we would formulate the answer to the question we have posed, as follows: Missions in the last three centuries have been a theological necessity, because the proclamation of the gospel in the world is always so. Therefore it was *not* a historical contingency but rather a *heilsgeschichtlich* progression of the word and work of God on earth. The theological necessity of the proclamation remains the same, but the *heilsgeschichtlich* hour has become *another* hour. And if we are not to weaken all too greatly the eschatological character of the time of the expectation of the fullness, we must also dare to say that the salvation of the world is *nearer* to us now than in the generations which were before us!

C. The third question is that concerning the specific significance of the preaching of the gospel in foreign lands. We begin once more with a word from Walter Freytag:

> Because Christian proclamation witnesses not only to the Kingdom which has come, but also to the Kingdom which is coming, foreign mission has abiding right amongst the task of proclamation in the space and range of our own Church. The Kingdom of God concerns the whole, and the view of the end embraces the whole world. The congregation which waits for the Lord cannot keep its nature if it lets itself be inclosed within the space of one people and does not participate in work and prayer in the proclamation among all nations.[22]

Alongside this passage we may cite a statement from the Evanston committee for the main theme of the second Assembly of the W.C.C.:

> How necessary it is, then, that the Church's obedience to the gospel should also involve a determination on the part of the Church in every country to take this gospel to other lands. There are frontiers which the gospel must cross within each land, areas of life which must be brought into subjection to the mind of Christ. But it is of special significance when the gospel crosses geographical frontiers, for it is when a Church takes the gospel to another people and another land

that it bears its witness to the fact that the new age has dawned for all the world.[23]

In the third place we refer to a statement by Max Warren, who sees the significance of foreign missions, particularly in the healing work of the gospel in

> a world deeply riven by the divisions of class and race, of nation and ideology: No Church can afford to be without the inspiration of a foreigner's obedience to the missionary imperative, just as no Church can itself be fully obedient to that imperative without being committed to a foreign mission.[24]

A. A. van Ruler typifies the special place of mission in this way: it has the intentional and positive *going* of people to people and of continent to continent.... Mission must be seen as the proclamation of the Kingdom of God as the Kingdom of Christ to each new people and in each new time. Thus time becomes historically understood from its *eschaton*: the Kingdom of God.[25]

Karl Barth describes mission as follows:

> "Mission", understood now in the narrower—which is, however, the real, original—sense of the word, means "sending", a sending out into the nations for the purpose of testifying to the gospel, that represents the root of existence and at the same time also the root of the whole task of the people of Christ. In the "Mission" the Church breaks out, sets out on its road (*poreuthentes*—Matt. 28: 19), and takes the step which is necessary to it in the very depths of its being, the step beyond its own self and also beyond its own environment (which from the Christian point of view raises so many problems) out into that humanity which is entrapped in so many false, wilful and powerless beliefs, and bound to so many false gods (false, because they simply reflect mankind's own glory and misery) of both older and newer invention and authority—that world of men who are still strangers to the word of God concerning His bond of mercy which also includes them, the word which in Jesus Christ was sent to them too. Therefore this word must first

be carried to man as a message new to him. The call which constitutes the community is precisely the command to carry this message to the world of men, to the nations, to the heathen. In that it obeys this command, the community is undertaking "mission to the heathen".[26]

Finally let me quote the statement of Paul S. Minear:

The unity of the Church can be seen as embodied in the activity of glorifying God with one voice (Rom. 15: 6) and the mission of the Church can be described as the method by which men, through enabling others to glorify God for His mercy (Rom. 15: 9), participate in the multiplication of thanksgiving to the glory of God (2 Cor. 4: 15).[27]

We have intentionally chosen definitions and formulations of the special nature of mission which have been given in the last few decades, and we have placed continental European, British, and American witnesses side by side.

Common to all is the linking of mission and eschatology. Here we could speak of a *communis opinio*. It is remarkable that only Freytag and Barth exhibit this eschatological feature in dark "*kulturcritisch*" (culture-critical) colours, while the others strike only the white keys. This is undoubtedly connected with the fact that for Freytag (and to a lesser degree also Barth) the element of expectation is dominant, while the others give more weight to the element of *fulfilment*. The distinction emerges most clearly between the formulation of Freytag and the Evanston statement; the eschatological accent seems to me weakest in Minear's statement. But we must take note of the fact that only Minear calls attention in his article to a feature which has thus far been greatly neglected, as regards the foundation and motivation of mission.[28]

To answer the question which concerns us at the moment, however, it is important that everyone should recognize the characteristic of mission to lie in *going out* to other *nations* (Freytag, Evanston report, Warren, van

Ruler), to other *men* who do not know God (Barth, Minear). If we are to understand the idea of "nations" in the purely Biblical sense, that is, in contrast with Israel, exclusively in the meaning of "men who do not know God", then we are no farther along toward an answer to the special question with which we are now dealing. The word "nations" really has, however, a secondary meaning, of "inhabitants of other countries". The accent falls on the geographical area as a typifying and even a constitutive element of mission. Furthermore, Freytag, Barth, and van Ruler obviously mean to make a distinction between the proclamation of the gospel to the de-Christianized environment and to those in the non-Christianized world.[29]

It seems to me that Freytag has made a decisive observation: "the congregation which waits for its Lord cannot keep its nature . . . if it lets itself be enclosed within the space of one people . . . if it does not participate in the proclamation *among all nations*." Christ's dominion over the world presses to a proclamation across *all* boundaries, because there are *no* boundaries for those who confess Christ as the Lord of the world and as the Hope of the world. Is there not something of an ideological shifting of emphases whenever the *ethnic-geographical* factors are brought to the forefront, or sometimes even substituted in place of the Biblical message of the intensive and extensive *universality* of salvation? Unconsciously and unintentionally, then, the old contrasts like East-West, white-coloured, primitive-developed, etc., begin to take on a greater role than they have in the Biblical witness. The *geographical* factor makes sense only as a sign of the recognition of Jesus Christ as the Saviour *of the world*.

The Evanston statement says that when the Church brings the joyous message to another land, she bears witness to the fact that the new age has dawned for the *whole* world. In the midst of the *boundaries* between groups, nations, and races, and over against the various powers, to witness to God, who has put everything under the feet of

Christ (Eph. 1: 22), means not only to have a share in being drawn into the struggle for the world, but also in the triumph of Christ. The knowledge of the power of His resurrection, as well as the fellowship in His suffering, is guaranteed to the apostolic Church (Phil. 3: 10). That is why the knowledge of Christ as Saviour of the world is the condition of the missionary activity which recognizes the *whole* world as "my parish". The reality of Jesus Christ as Saviour and Hope of the world is not only a matter of faith, it is *also* a matter of seeing that Christ builds His community as a community among *all* nations. Therefore the Church which is faithful to her Lord (in witness, service, and thanksgiving) will search the horizons to continue to discover new signs of the Kingdom of God in the midst of this world.

Whoever has seen Christ cannot do other than see the world, and whoever sees the world also sees the *map* of the world. This is equally valid for both older and younger Churches. The Church is a witness of Christ in the world, or else she is not an obedient Church of Christ. She is the light of the world, the salt of the earth (Matt. 5: 14, 13).

We shall, however, have to detach ourselves, in so far as we are concerned with the foundation and motivation of mission, from the typical eighteenth- and nineteenth-century associations which expressions like "all nations" and the "ends of the earth" called forth. Only *then* and *thus* is the geographical component a legitimate component for mission.

3. Church and Mission

Particularly in the last ten years there has been much discussion in missionary circles of "Church and mission". This discussion need not detain us here since it has been described elsewhere.[30] But we shall have to discuss the question of the extent to which the *Biblical investigation* gives us the occasion and the right to contrast Church and mission. Thus far in the discussion we have been more led by the historical growth of the state of affairs than by the light of the gospel. But a remarkable development has taken place in Biblical theology in the last few decades which has led to the rediscovery of the Church as a community of the Kingdom, as a witnessing and serving community in and for the world. Outside the existing missionary movement, the conviction that the Church is a missionary Church or it is no Church is accepted by the great majority. The centuries-old ecclesiology which has remained 'so static is now gradually being replaced by a more dynamic one which is both eschatological and missionary.

Is there, in the light of the present state of theology of the Old and New Testament, any occasion to speak of a separate "theology of mission"? One can maintain this, it seems to me, *only* if one misunderstands the Church as well as mission. It appears to me that the studies mentioned in Chapter 1 regarding election as election *for service* have opened the way to a new insight into the being and calling of the Church. The Church which has been chosen out of the world is chosen for this end—that she performs for the world the service of giving witness to the Kingdom of God which has come and is coming in Jesus Christ. If theology is really *theo-logia*—a speaking about *God*, then she cannot do otherwise than speak of the God who "is not a statue but an overflowing fountain of good".[31] The triune God who is involved with the world in the *sending* of the prophets, of Jesus Christ, and of the Holy Spirit, also sends the apostles and the Church.[32] I think that it would be a "back-translation" into old and theologically abandoned categories, if one were to vindicate the "theology of mission" as a separate field of theology. "Segregation" is always a precarious affair in a world which has been brought by the saving activity of God "under one Head".

It is no coincidence that in the last thirty years there has been a recognition that the unity of the ecumenical and the missionary movements is a unity theologically justified and commanded. "To fill the world with the message of Christ, is a task beyond the power of individual Churches. And victory and defeat of the individual Churches in this service is the victory of us all and the defeat of us all."[33] There is a remarkable coincidence between theological development and historical occurrences. They work on each other and they strengthen each other.

The unity between Church and mission, the unity, that is, between mission as a service of the Church and the Church as sent into the world, does not mean that there is no longer room for a basic reflection regarding the *conditions* and *manner* and *extent* of the service of the Church to the world. But every separate "theology of mission" will make acute the old danger of the separation of things which God has joined together in His Word. This can be nothing but a source of difficulties and problems.[34]

When we see the unity of "Church and mission" in Biblical light, then I think the misunderstanding that there are two stages, first the stage of mission, and after that the stage of the Church, will disappear. I remember a slogan from Dutch student circles: "Mission out, the world-church in". One must allow students such shouts, but at the same time we must do our utmost to liberate them from this ideological distortion of "mission" as well as of the "world-church".

There is no other Church than the Church *sent* into the world, and there is no other mission than that of the Church of Christ. The consequence for theology, I think, is that a theological reflection of missionary service *is* possible and extremely necessary, but not a "theology of missions".

We must now return to an expression used by Bishop Stephen Neill, quoted earlier in this chapter, which has almost become a slogan in the discussion of a "theology of missions"—"If everything is mission, nothing, is mission".

We should not pass too lightly over the phrase "if every-thing is mission". The conviction is indeed gaining ground that everything that the community of Christ does on earth should be considered in the light of its "mission". This conviction is far from being expressed in the practical attitude and acts of the Church. Many Churches are characterized by "nothing is mission" rather than by "everything is mission".

The one-sidedness with which the eschatological func-tion of missionary work as "foreign mission(s)" has been emphasized in the missionary thinking of the past few decennia can, however, help the Church in finding itself again as Church-in-the-world and Church-for-the-world, in its fresh encounter with the world which the Church has been called upon to face everywhere.

If one wants to maintain a specifically theological mean-ing of the term mission as "foreign mission(s)", its signifi-cance is, in my opinion, that it keeps calling the Church to think over its essential nature as a community sent forth into the world. Seen in that light missionary work is not just one of its activities, but the *criterion for all its activities*. Missionary work reflects in a unique way, particularly in its passing of boundaries in space and spirit, the very essence of the Church as a Church. It returns (as it were) to its origin, and is confronted with its basis and its justi-fication by being confronted with its missionary calling. It is exactly by going outside itself that the Church *is* itself and comes to itself.

> This complete reflection of the life of the Church in its missionary work will keep it from becoming introspective and introverted, from becoming narrow-minded and small-minded, for it brings it into contact with the complete life of the world.[35]

"Whether Paul, or Apollos, or Cephas, or the world, or life, or death, or things present, or things to come; all are yours; and ye are Christ's; and Christ is God's" (I Cor.

3: 22, 23). These words express the privilege and the right, the calling and the joy of the Church as Christ's servant. It is at one and the same time the secret of its being sent forth into the world and of its being independent of "old and new" situations in missionary work.

The days when missionary work was the Cinderella of the Church seem to be past. When, in 1950, the Reformed Church of the Netherlands took over the work of the various missionary societies that had lived and worked independent of the official Church since 1800, the then managing director of missions, Dr. K. J. Brouwer, used the following figure of speech. Once missionary work, though the legitimate child of the Church, was abandoned by the Church. Now the one-time foundling is again adopted as its legitimate and beloved child.

He who studies the history of the missionary work of the past few centuries cannot escape the impression that practically everywhere in Europe and America missionary work has been treated more as a foundling than as a legitimate child. It is not superfluous to ask whether in again being accepted by the official Church its *strangeness* has been overcome.

Could it not be that this strangeness is inherent in missionary work, just because it, and it in particular, represents the Church in its real and essential shape as the Church which has been sent forth into the world? Christ's Church is in *this* world as a sign of and a summons to the *world to come*, a phenomenon which is so impossible that it is always in danger of losing its own nature. It has been said of Jesus Christ that He is "a sign which shall be spoken against" (Luke 2: 34). The Church of Christ, which is simultaneously His body and His servant, shares with Him that it is spoken against.

This contradiction does not come from outside only but also from inside. It has been the great temptation for the Church throughout all ages to conform to this world. If it does, it becomes just another society, a "club for religious folk-lore" (Hoekendijk). During the past few centuries missionary work has again and again fulfilled in the "old Christian countries" the task of rebelling in a positive sense against all institutional, denominational and religious rigidity and against the desire to conform to the powers of this world. It will only be able to go on doing so in future if it manages to withdraw itself from the suction power of this conformity. The conservatism and rigidity of many missionary corporations that were once alive and mobile, the smell of colonialism which makes the atmosphere of many old mission posts unbearable, are so many proofs of how great the suction power of conformity is.

> We must accept the facts as they are, and give up every defensive attitude. The missions are in danger in the same way as the Churches. We are always tempted to identify our empirical, human and therefore imperfect realizations, in this case the empirical Church, as it is, and the empirical missions, as they are, with the Church we believe, and with the Mission, which is commanded to us. What was in former times a historic expression of true obedience, becomes then independent and looses itself from the nature of obedience and hampers the new expression of that obedience which is required from us today.[36]

Man who is "no longer a Christian" and man who is "not yet a Christian", both belong to the world that needs the gospel and for whom it is intended. That is why Churches everywhere in the world can understand each other better and better, why they *should* understand each other better and better in the service of witnessing.

In this situation the apostleship of Paul, which is unusual and in a sense irregular as compared with the regular apostleship of the twelve, who represent eschatological Israel, can give us a new outlook (cf. Chapter 6, §3). The great significance of the gospel, which was to renew life and the world, became clear to him *just because* he was the apostle of the Gentiles. It was mainly Paul's epistles to the Gentile Christian communities that revealed the real nature of both the community of Christ and the world. Humanly speaking the Christian Church would without Paul have remained a Jewish sect. Is it too far-fetched to assume that it is also because Paul's apostleship had brought the whole world within their horizon that the authors of the four Gospels (which were all written later than Paul's epistles!) had them culminate in the description of a task that encompasses the whole world? Have they not also come to a better understanding of the import of Jesus' words and work through the expansion of the Church over all of the world that lay within their horizon, the *oecumene*?

These are questions to which the answers lie far beyond the scope of this study. There is no doubt, however, that Paul's reflection of the gospel is the fruit of his missionary activities (1 Cor. 15: 10). The "irregular" apostle has done more work than all the other apostles, even though he does not give himself credit for it but ascribes it to "the grace of God that was bestowed upon me". The ex-centricity that is characteristic of Paul's apostleship has a deep meaning also for the missionary task of the present. Just as to Paul the light arose over the mystery of the salvation of all humanity (Eph. 3: 4–6) which had not been known to previous generations, so the Church of today will not be able to understand the "divine economy" (Eph. 3: 9) in any other way, nor preach the mystery (Eph. 3: 9) in any other way than by its continued "preparation of the gospel of peace" (Eph. 6: 15). Missionary work is like a pair of sandals that have been given to the Church in order that it shall set out on the road and *keep on going* to make known the mystery of the gospel (Eph. 6: 19). Only thus will this mystery be revealed more and more to the Church itself. Serving among the Gentiles enabled Paul to serve the Church; the Church *lives* mainly on his *missionary* epistles!

Perhaps the missionary service of the Church will only be given a more or less "irregular" place in future, and many may continue to regard the emphasis on the fact that the Church was *sent forth* into the world as something ex-centric, even as something incidental. Let missionary work remain aware of its charismatic nature in an activity and mobility that are as great as possible in order that of missionary work, too, it can be said that "I laboured more abundantly than they all: yet not I, but the grace of God which was with me" (1 Cor. 15: 10).

Let us not forget that the great prime mover of the preaching of the gospel does not come from outside (the "need of the world") and not from within either (the "religious impulse") but from above, as a divine coercion —"woe is unto me, if I preach not the gospel!" (1 Cor. 9: 16), as a matter of life and death, not for the world, but for the Church itself—"And this I do for the gospel's sake, that I might be partaker thereof with you" (1 Cor. 9: 23).

Epilogue: The Miracle of the Community

Let us now in conclusion summarize the results of our investigation. In order to remain faithful to the character of this survey as a summary of the *Biblical* data regarding the foundation and the motivation of mission, however, we will not formulate a number of theses, but keep to the word of the Bible itself.

In a somewhat more detailed exegesis of the well-known passage 1 Pet. 2: 9–10, we will, then, illustrate the purpose of the argument in the previous paragraph, viz. that a "theology of mission" cannot be other than a "theology of the Church" as the people of God called *out* of the world, placed *in* the world, and sent *to* the world. This passage is as follows: "But you are a chosen race, a royal priesthood, a holy nation, a people for God's own possession, that you may declare the wonderful deeds of him who called you out of darkness into his marvellous light. Once you were no people but now you are God's people; once you had not received mercy but now you have received mercy."[37]

A. The first letter of Peter is characterized by an eschatological trait, and by a word usage which is closely connected with that of the Old Testament. "There is no book in the New Testament where the eschatology is more closely integrated with the teaching of the document as a whole."[38]

Verses 9–10 form the climax and the closing of the pericope 2:1–10. Jesus Christ is called the corner-stone by the use of an image borrowed from Isa. 28:16. Whoever builds his faith on Him will not be put to shame, 2:6. But not everyone believes that, besides being the corner-stone, Jesus Christ is also the stone that will make men stumble and the rock that will make them fall, 2:8. There is a disobedience to the word on the part of many. We are referring here to the people of Israel which Jesus Christ has rejected, as well as to the Gentiles who have rejected the gospel. The letter is in the first place directed to the Gentile Christians "in the dispersion", 1:1. Verses 9–10 proceed from the great contrast between those who reject the gospel and the Church which has accepted it. The description of the Church bears the character of a hymn. In this hymn of praise, man comes to his destiny, and with him the whole creation (cf. Rom. 11:25–26, 14:11, 15:7–13). This description of the Church, however, does not bear an impersonal, contemplative character. The Church is not *spoken* of as an objective entity, but is *addressed* as the community which believes in Jesus Christ.

Can one, may one, really speak about the Church in any other way than in a praising and glorifying address to the Church herself? *But you*—who are you?

In four expressions it is stated who one is if he believes in Christ. These expressions are all borrowed from the Old Testament. In other words, they are designations which were given to Israel from of old. But this means it is clearly indicated that the community of Jesus Christ participates in and may bear the names of Israel. Those who believe in Jesus Christ from Israel are the true Israel, and those who come to Him from the Gentiles are incorporated into Israel.

The names of Israel, borrowed from Exod. 19: 5–6, Isa. 43: 20, 61: 6, make it clear once and for all that God's plan for the world is not frustrated by the disobedience of Israel, but that it is being fulfilled in the fact that the Church is taking the place of Israel and receives the honour of Israel. Only in Christ does Israel come to her right; to put it even more strongly—only in the community of Christ do God's intentions for Israel become quite clear.

To gain a full understanding of the significance and range of the four designations of the community, we must take account of the fact that they are most emphatically and intentionally *in a final context*: the Greek *hopōs* (which is stronger than the usual *pōs*) must not be neglected or weakened in any respect. Perhaps it can best be rendered by the translation: in order that you *thus, with the qualifications here stated*, may proclaim the great acts of Him who has called you. In Christian usage the designations which occur here have often been applied to the Church herself, as if she had a valid right to these designations apart from the purpose for which they have here been given. In other words: only as a community which understands the purpose for which it has received the lovely names of Israel may it really appropriate these names. The "(in order) that" in verse 9, is the hinge on which the door turns that gives entrance to the treasures which lie piled up in these names. "In the progress of verse 9 there is talk of proclamation. In this way it becomes clear that all the designations stated, as well as those implied in the *hierateuma* (priesthood), are limited not only to the inner Christian fellowship, as often happens in the common Christian usage of the 'general priesthood', but also that they are to be considered as a service of witness (in the sense of Isa. 61: 6—cf. verse 9) for mankind."[39]

Only when we remember this directedness to the "service of witness for mankind" is it possible for us to understand what is characteristic of the community of Christ. What does this mean except that the Church of Jesus Christ has the right, solely as a *missionary Church*, to call herself "Church" at all? She is assaulting the salvation of God when she usurps these titles "for her own use".

B. Let us look more closely at the designations in the light of the service of witness for mankind which we have had in view.

"*You are a chosen race.*" This expression has been borrowed from Isa. 43: 20, and is used to typify Christians in the New Testament only here—that is to say, the word "race". The word (Greek: *genos*) here means "nation", with the accent on origin. This origin lies in the *world out of which* election has taken place. The miracle and the riddle of election, which Israel has been neither able nor willing to understand, still exists. Whoever is offended by the election of Israel as one particular nation out of all others will *also* be offended by the Church of Jesus Christ. God does not undo the fact of election. Must not this Israelite designation be a sign that God has always *remained* the God of Israel?

In the community of Christ as a chosen race, there now emerges the intention of God's plan for Israel as an election for *service* to the world: you are a chosen race, called out of the world, in order to proclaim the great acts of God *in* the world.

"*You are a royal priesthood.*" The expression has been borrowed from Exod. 19: 6, and says positively what "chosen race" has said negatively: the Church of Christ is chosen for a royal priesthood.[40]

The priesthood receives the major emphasis; it is more closely defined by "royal". In Old Testament usage, certainly in the usage of Exod. 19: 6, the meaning of priesthood is not in the first place to indicate the service of sacrifice, but the mediating of divine instruction and directives for living to the whole people. In this way the priest stood in a certain sense *over against* the people, because he stood "before God's face" on behalf of the people. The word "priesthood" is however applied here to the community of Christ as a whole. In view of the "service of witness for the world", one must here take it to mean that the Church of Christ as a whole stands before God serving. By serving in dedication to God, she is enabled to do priestly service in the world: her serving God *is* service to the world, because God is not now to be detached from His world! He is not just "simply-God", "God-in-Himself", but is the God of His people and the God of the whole earth. The *deus otiosus* of the Gentiles and the god of the philosophers are *alone*, in themselves, for themselves; but the God of Abraham and Jacob, the living God (Matt. 22: 32), is never *without* men. Therefore the priestly serving of Him is also service to His world; it is witness to the gospel that "God so loved the world, that he gave his only begotten Son". By belonging to God in *this* kind of priestly service, the new people of God also receives the predicate "royal". This means first of all that this people has God as king, but also that they share in His royal glory. Man is royal man, *because* he is God's man, in His image, in His likeness.

The priestly serving of God is service in royal freedom; here priesthood and kingship interpenetrate reciprocally, as in Jesus Christ Himself. This royal freedom of the priestly service exists for the sake of witness in the world; yes, the life of the community as a royal priesthood is already a witness in itself. The proclamation of the marvellous deeds of God occurs not only by word and deed; it already takes place in the existence of the community.

"*You are a holy nation.*" The expression used here is a wholly unusual combination of *nation* (in the sense of belonging to the world of nations or Gentiles—Greek *ethnos*, Hebrew *gôy*) and *holy*. In the Old Testament the combination was always of "holy" with "the people of Israel". Both Hebrew and Greek have a special word for *people* (Israel) and people (nation, Gentiles). Here the predicate of Israel (holy) is combined with the word for "Gentiles". This must be understood first of all as an indication that the community of the Gentiles has taken over the place of Israel; this antithetic tendency, as we have already seen, is not alien to the first letter of Peter and particularly to the pericope 2: 1–10. But it further suggests the positive intention that the Gentiles, unholy in themselves, have been sanctified by coming to Christ. By this means they have separated themselves from the others, the disobedient, and now stand in a positive relation to God. Although the cultic character that is at bottom peculiar to the Hebrew and the Greek words (*qādhôš* and *hagios* respectively) may have been weakened and spiritualized, nevertheless it is not lacking here altogether. The community from the world of nations is *also* a cultus community, separated for service to God. One might say that the expression "holy nation" is here a further definition of the word "priesthood". The community is not only priest, but also a temple of God in the spirit (cf. also 1 Pet. 2: 5, Eph. 2: 22).

A "holy Gentile people" is really a contradiction, but this human impossibility has been made a divine reality in Christ.

"*You are a people for God's possession.*" In contrast to the previous expression, "a holy nation", this word which is now used is a technical term in the New Testament for Israel (Greek *laos*, Hebrew *'am*). The use of *both* words for the same community again underlines the fact that the dividing wall which separates has been broken down in Christ (cf. Eph. 2: 14).

But the addition of "for God's possession" says something else: the community of Christ can only be God's people because He Himself has made her His possession. The Greek word and the context (*eis peripoiēsin*) suggest an active intervention of God Himself: the dynamic of love which acquires and keeps His possession: "No one is able to snatch them out of my hand; no one is able to snatch anything out of my Father's hand" (John 10: 28, 29).

One man might give names to every living being (Gen. 2: 19): now *God* gives names to His community, and this name-giving is a seal on ownership. We may see, then, in the names here received nothing less than a sealing, a confirmation of the Church of Christ. So *was* she in God's thoughts in time of old, so *is* she now in and for the world, so *shall* she be in the completion of the ages.

C. "*That you may declare the wonderful deeds of him who called you.*"

We have already referred to the particularly heavy emphasis the "(in order) to" (Greek *hopōs*) receives in the context. Only *as* the chosen race, *as* the royal priesthood, *as* the holy nation, *as* God's own people is the Church of Christ called and able to proclaim the wonderful deeds of God. What is more, she can be a chosen race only in and through this proclamation, and only thus does she appear to be so.

It is really incomprehensible that so often in the history of the Christian Church this clear and obvious statement has not been understood in its unity-duality, but has been split apart, or even that the proclamation of the wonderful deeds of God has been confined merely to a hymn of praise behind thick church walls. No doubt the "churchly" hymn of praise is also asked and intended. The praise of God in the sense of creation and thankfulness is closely connected with praise.[41] But the true praise is not only an internal Christian affair; it is witness in and for the world. In the praise of the community of Christ, God (finally) receives from His world the answer which He has awaited from the beginning, as the human echo to His divine approval (the "very good" of Gen. 1: 31) of the work of His hands.[42]

But we must not remain too long with the raising of songs of praise in the narrower sense. The real praise is the declaration of the wonderful deeds of God in the world. These deeds (Greek *aretē*) are the only deeds spoken of in the community of Christ; the deeds by which He has carried through His plan for the world; the deeds which are indicated in the four names by which the community of Christ has just been addressed. The proclamation of the gospel in the world can, may, and must never be anything else than the speaking of the deeds of *God*. As soon as the Church of Christ starts proclaiming other deeds than God's deeds, she is unfaithful and can no longer be a blessing and a service to the world. Herein there also lies an adverse judgment against all motives for mission which have played a role in history, either as major or minor motives. We cannot be careful enough of the *motive* for mission. Perhaps one may on the other hand venture to say that the motive of the proclamation of God's wonderful deeds is so broad and powerful that it overshadows all other motives.

Although it is obviously not necessary for the writer of the first letter of Peter to specify in detail what he means by the transparent self-revelation of God in His deeds (this is perhaps the best rendering of the word *aretē*), nevertheless he gives some further indication in the next phrase, "who *called* you out of darkness". It has been a *calling* of God by which the community has come into being, the same creative calling by which He once called the world into being (cf. Ps. 33: 9).

In Christ a new creation has arisen. The world must *hear* from the community of Christ that the new world of God has begun. The "chosen race, the royal priesthood, the holy nation, the people of God's own possession" is itself the beginning of this new world. And the "loud proclamation" of the Church is a continuation of the calling of God. Just as God's sending of the Son continues in the sending of the Spirit and the sending of the community into the world (John 20: 21), so the calling of God continues in the proclamation of the Church. This proclamation is of course nothing else but making known what this calling of God has amounted to.

"*Out of the darkness into his marvellous light.*" The darkness is the alienation from God. It stands here as the undefined, the unbound (the article is lacking) over against the *one*, only light (the article has special power in connection with the possessive pronoun). The surprising and astonishing aspect of this calling to the light evokes wonder at the admirable offer.

"*Once you were no people but now you are God's people.*" These and the following words have been borrowed from Hos. 1: 6–11, 2: 23. There the "*lō-'ammi*" has reference only to Israel; here the prophetic work is also applied to the Gentiles: the Gentile Christians receive Israel's inheritance even in the fact that they may view the word of the prophet as directed to *them*. In Christ the Scriptures are opened (cf. Luke 24: 25, 27, 32, 2 Cor. 3: 14–16) to the Gentiles, just as they are closed for Israel because she rejects Christ. This surprising use of Scripture also belongs to the marvellous light to which God calls His community. Therefore the Old Testament, though it appears to speak chiefly of Israel, is of such outstanding significance for the community of Christ.

By the application of the word from Hosea, "not-my-people", it is further made clear that God's disappointment over Israel has really been His disappointment over *all* nations, and the judgment which Israel has sustained by her apostasy has been the judgment of *all*.

The darkness out of which God has called the community by Christ is thus the darkness of being "not-my-people"; cf. Eph. 2: 12, "separated from Christ, that is, alienated from the commonwealth of Israel, and strangers to the covenants of promise, having no hope and without God in the world". The light is fellowship with God, the fact of having "been brought nigh in the blood of Christ" (Eph. 2: 13). The "formerly, but *now*" accentuates all the more the great contrast between formerly and the meaning (which changes everything) of the eschatological hour "now".

In God's nearness the life of fellowship begins to flourish too, so that the community of Christ drawn from all nations can rightly be called a "people" (or nation). All other national community in the world can be nothing but a reflex of *this* fellowship. In the light of this being a "people of God", our belonging to any other nation becomes supremely unimportant; and a man can be a blessing within any other specific nation only when he remains faithful to his citizenship in the people of God. God's marvellous light also conquers the "powers" of nationalism, like all other powers which would overcome the light (cf. John 1: 5).

"*Once you had not received mercy but now you have received mercy.*" These words are also borrowed from the prophecy of Hosea, and they repeat what has already been said in regard to "not-my-people" and God's people. Further, this repetition characterizes in another way the contents of the proclamation of God's marvellous deeds. The pity, the grace, of God is to the community of Christ what light is for the earth. The darkness of alienation from God has lasted *long* (the perfect participle has a pluperfect meaning and indicates the long duration of a situation), but *now* God's pity becomes living and powerful in Christ over the newly accepted people of God. (The aorist of "accepted" has an inchoative sense.) The long night is passed and the day has dawned.

As long as it is day, the community of Christ may and must proclaim the deeds of God, and therewith, in her turn, call men out of darkness into light; out of alienation into true fellowship with God and man; out of a twilight situation of mercilessness into the joy of mercy.

So long as there are in this world men in darkness, without God and without mercy, so long will the task of mission of the Christian Church endure. But she can complete this only when she remains powerfully conscious that she herself shared in the same darkness and alienation, and that out of this she is called to proclaim to others the marvellous deeds of the God of light, fellowship, and mercy. There is no other "theology of mission", no other oracle, than this.

NOTES

Introduction

1. *The Ghana Assembly of the International Missionary Council*, edited by R. K. Orchard, Edinburgh House Press, London 1958, p. 138.

2. A survey of, and an insight into, the variety of motives for mission is given, for Great Britain, by J. v. d. Berg, *Constrained by Jesus' Love, An Inquiry into the Motives of the Missionary Awakening in Great Britain in the Period between 1698 and 1815*, J. H. Kok, Kampen 1956. For Germany in the second half of the nineteenth century: Seppo A. Teinonen, *Gustav Warneckin varhaisen läketysteorian teologiset perusteet*, Helsinki 1959. This work, written in the Finnish language, was accessible to me only in the English summary, pp. 238-58. By the same writer there is: *Warneck Tutkielmia*, Helsinki 1959, with a summary in German, pp. 47-56. For the motives for missions on the European continent, see further: Joh. Dürr, *Sendende und Werdende Kirche in der Missionstheologie Gustav Warnecks*, Basler Missions Buchhandlung, Basel 1947; J. C. Hoekendijk, *Kerk en Volk in de Duitse Zendingsweten-schap*, Ned. Zendingsraad, Amsterdam 1948.

3. See the little work of H. Schärer, strongly influenced by the theology of K. Barth: *Die Begründung der Mission in der katholischen und evangelischen Missionswissenschaft*, Theol. Studien, Heft 16, Zollikon Verlag, Zürich 1944; Joh. Dürr, *Die Reinigung der Missionsmotive*, EMM, 1951.

4. On the relation of theology to mission in general, see O. G. Myklebust, *The Study of Missions in Theological Education*, Egede Institutte, Oslo, I 1955, II 1957. Further: O. Kübler, *Mission und Theologie, Eine Untersuchung über den Missionsgedanken in der systematischen Theologie seit Schleiermacher*, T. C. Hinrichsche Buchhandlung, Leipzig 1929; E. zur Nieden, *Der Missionsgedanke in der systematischen Theologie seit Schleiermacher*, Bertelsmann, Gütersloh 1928. I am not acquainted with similar summarizing works for Great Britain and North America.

Chapter 1

1. For this older literature, see for example E. Riehm, *Der Missionsgedanke im Alten Testament*, AMZ, 1880; M. Löhr, *Der Missionsgedanke im Alten Testament*, A. K. Verlagsbuchhandlung J. C. B. Mohr, Freiburg, Leipzig 1896; A. Bertholet, *Die Stellung der Israeliten und der*

Juden zu den Fremden, Tübingen, J. C. B. Mohr, 1896; B. Kleinpaul, *Die Mission in der Bibel*, H. G. Wallmann, Leipzig 1901; E. Sellin, *Der Missionsgedanke im Alten Testament*, NAMZ, 1925; W. Staerk, *Ursprung und Grenzen der Missionskraft der alttestamentlichen Religion*, Theol. Blätter IV, 1925; J. Reinhard, *Der Heilsuniversalismus der Bibel*, NAMZ, 1926; F. M. Th. Böhl, *Oud-Israël en de Zending*, Mededeelingen, Tijdschrift voor Zendingswetenschap, Oegstgeest 1929. From English language material the following older works are known to me: W. O. Carver, *The Bible as a Missionary Message*, Revell, New York 1921; H. A. Lapham, *The Bible as a Missionary Handbook*, Heffer, Cambridge 1925.

2. E.g. J. Pedersen, *Israel*, Oxford Univ. Press 1926 (I, II), 1940 (III, IV), Copenhagen; L. Köhler, *Theologie des Alten Testaments*, 1936 (E.T. *Old Testament Theology*); J. Hempel, *Gott und Mensch im Alten Testament*, 2, Kohlhammer, Stuttgart 1936; O. Procksch, *Theologie des Alten Testaments*, Bertelsmann, Gütersloh 1950; Th. C. Vriezen, *Hoofdlijnen der Theologie van het Oude Testament*, 2, H. Veenman, Wageningen 1955 (E.T. *Old Testament Theology*); E. Jacob, *Théologie de l'Ancien Testament*, Delachaux & Niestlé, Neuchâtel & Paris 1956 (E.T. *The Theology of the Old Testament*), and others. In Great Britain and North America introductions from the point of view of historical criticism are preponderant; so, for example, H. E. Fosdick, *A Guide to the Understanding of the Bible*, Harper Bros., New York, and London, 1938; R. H. Pfeiffer, *Introduction to the Old Testament*, Harper Bros., New York, and London, 1941; the works of W. F. Albright. But on the other hand, note G. D. Wright, *The Challenge of Israel's Faith*, 2nd ed., Univ. of Chicago Press 1946. Closer to the continental European development stands H. H. Rowley. See, e.g., his *The Biblical Doctrine of Election*, Lutterworth Press, London 1950, 1953; *The Unity of the Bible*, Carey Kingsgate Press, London 1953; *The Faith of Israel*, S.C.M. Press, London 1956.

3 *Op. cit.*, p. 114. "Historical research seeks a critically guaranteed minimum; the kerygmatic image tends to a theological maximum."

4. *Op. cit.*, p. 126.

5. See the works already cited of S. A. Teinonen and also, for example, W. Kunze, *Der Missionsgedanke bei J. T. Beck*, EMM, 1930.

6. Here reference is also to the Biblicism of J. A. Bengel, J. T. Beck *et al*. See R. B. Evenhuis, *De biblizistisch-eschatologische Theologie von J. A. Bengel*, H. Veenman, Wageningen 1931. Critique of this theology in G. von Rad, *Theologie des Alten Testaments* II, Ch. Kaiser Verlag, Munich 1960, p. 375 (E.T. in preparation, *Theology of the Old Testament*).

7. K. Hartenstein, *Heidentum und Kirche*, EMM, 1936, p. 5.

8. I hope I may be excused from the duty of listing all accessible

commentaries. Surely of special significance for *our* purpose is the explication of Gen. 1–11 in G. von Rad, *Das erste Buch Mose, Kap. 1–12: 9*, "Das Alte Testament Deutsch", Teilband 2, Vandenhoeck & Rupprecht, Göttingen 1950 (E.T. *Genesis*). Further mention must be made of W. Eichrodt, *Theologie des Alten Testaments*, Abhandlungen zur Theologie des Alten und Neuen Testaments, No. 4, 2nd ed., Evangelische Verlagsanstalt, Berlin 1948 (E.T. *Theology of the Old Testament*). See also F. J. Leenhardt, *La Situation de l'Homme d'après le Genèse*, in *Das Menschenbild im Lichte des Evangeliums, Festschrift E. Brunner*, Zwingli Verlag, Zürich 1950, pp. 1–30; W. Zimmerli, *Die Urgeschichte*, Erster Teil, Zwingli Verlag, Zürich 1943; etc.

9. Besides G. von Rad, *Theologie des Alten Testaments* (see note 6 above), we may mention Th. C. Vriezen, *Onderzoek naar de Paradijsvoor-stelling bij de oude Semietische Volken*, H. Veenman, Wageningen 1957, p. 17, etc. Counter to the habit accepted in the last half century of separating Gen. 1–11 as "primeval history" (German, *Urgeschichte*) from the historical portions of the Old Testament, there has arisen a resistance under the influence of the "form criticism" type of exegesis of the Old Testament and of *heilsgeschichtliche* exegesis. We must not forget that these early chapters of Genesis also deal with the God who rules, leads, and turns history. At this point see K. Cramer, *Gen. 1–11 Urgeschichte?*, J. C. B. Mohr, Tübingen 1959; P. Morant, *Die Anfänge der Menschheit*, Räber & Cy., Lucerne 1960 (R.C.).

10. Because this whole section of the Bible is written in the light of the fact of the alienation between God (the God of Israel, Yahweh) and man, the world of nations, one is forced to these chapters in coming to an answer to the difficult question of the relation between religion and revelation. In the extensive literature, I believe not enough attention has heretofore been paid to this problem. It would repay our effort, it seems to me, to approach the issue (which is becoming more and more acute because of the renaissance of the old religions) of the relation of religion and revelation from the data in Gen. 1–12. Nowhere else in the Old Testament is the bond with God, the alienation of man from God, and God's constant covenantship with man more deeply and minutely professed than here. For the theological anthropology in my opinion the best and most penetrating book is still E. Brunner, *Der Mensch im Widerspruch*, Zwingli Verlag, Zürich 1937 (E.T. *Man in Revolt*).

11. See G. von Rad, *Theologie des Alten Testaments*, I, p. 168.

12. See H. H. Rowley, *The Missionary Message of the Old Testament*, Carey Kingsgate Press, London, pp. 24–26; and his *The Biblical Doctrine of Election*, pp. 65–67.

13. I have referred to another aspect of the primeval history of Gen. 1–11, in *The Mission of the People of God*, in *The Missionary Church*

in East and West, ed. by Ch. C. West and D. M. Paton, S.C.M. Press, London 1959, pp. 91–93.

14. See R. Martin-Achard, *Israel et les Nations, La Perspective Missionnaire de l'Ancien Testament*, Cahiers Théologiques 42, Delachaux & Niestlé, Neuchâtel & Paris 1959, p. 33. Those who translate "bless themselves" in Gen. 12: 3, instead of "will be blessed", also recognize the great significance of this declaration. The minimum is certainly stated in the words "something like the note of universalism is already struck in these words". C. F. North, *The Old Testament Interpretation of History*, Epworth Press, London 1946, p. 26.

15. H. H. Rowley, *The Biblical Doctrine of Election*, 3rd ed., 1953.

16. Rowley, *op. cit.*, p. 39.

17. Another who is opposed to the "fitness" of Israel is N. W. Porteous, *Volk und Gottesvolk im Alten Testament*, in *Theologische Aufsätze, Festschrift K. Barth*, Ch. Kaiser Verlag, Munich 1936, pp. 146–163. Cf. also my *Goden en Mensen*, J. C. Niemeyer, Groningen 1950, pp. 11–18.

18. Rowley, *op. cit.*, p. 52.

19. Zwingli Verlag, Zürich 1953.

20. Vriezen, *op. cit.*, p. 32; a particularly important study, which, more than the work of Rowley, also investigates word usage in the Old Testament regarding election.

21. *Ibid.*, p. 34.

22. For this Jewish distortion of the doctrine of election see, among others, C. Boess, *Altsynagogale Palestinische Theologie und Mission*, Alg. Miss. Zeitung, 1885, pp. 190 ff.; K. H. Miskotte, *Het Wezen der Joodse Religie*, H. J. Paris, Amsterdam 1933.

23. This observation is from Th. C. Vriezen, *op. cit.*, p. 50, who also points out that in Deutero-Isaiah *bāḥîr* is a nominal form which is often used for names of an office and therefore also has more of an active than a passive meaning. Compare also the declaration on p. 33: "Therefore Christian dogmatics can treat of those who are chosen (passive), whereas this is unknown to the Old Testament."

24. On the notions of "people" and "nation" in relation to the Old Testament, see G. Bertram in the entry "ethnos" in TWNT II, p. 362; L. Rost, *Die Bezeichnungen für Land und Volk im Alten Testament, Festschrift O. Procksch*, A. Deichert & J. C. Hinrichs, Leipzig 1934; W. Eichrodt, *Gottes Volk und die Völker*, EMM, 1942, speaks of a "yes" of God to the nationality (*Volkstum*) of Israel while at the same time God speaks à "no" to the nationality of the heathen. This otherwise absorbing and instructive article would have gained in worth, to my way of thinking, if Eichrodt had confined himself to the *heilsgeschichtliche* opposition between *'am* and *gōy*, Israel and the heathen, instead of operating with the doubtful concept of "nationality", which comes

out of Germanic rather than Biblical thinking. G. v. d. Leeuw, *Phaenomenologie der Religion*, *1*, J. C. B. Mohr, Tübingen 1933, 2nd ed. 1956, even names the Jewish people as the first historical example of a nation, but he thoroughly distorts the Biblical witness in regard to the people Israel, in my opinion, by so doing. See also my *Goden en Mensen* (note 17 above), pp. 7–10.

The proper statement of affairs has been made with particular clarity, I believe, by K. Emmerich, *Die Juden*, Theologische Studien und Kritiken 7, 1939, p. 20: "But the children of Israel are a people only in so far as they are a people of God. This means that neither a natural bond nor human will and realization has linked these people together, but only the establishment of a fellowship. It means further that to this nation the option is not open, to want to become a nation like other nations, since it did not become a nation the way other nations did. It means finally that this nation lives—should it wish to become a nation like others—under the threat that God will cease to call it 'my people' and will call it 'not my people'. If God should recognize this nation as His no longer, then it becomes a non-people, for only as the people of God did they become a people, or remain so."

25. For the investigation of the meaning of the "people of God", see G. von Rad, *Das Gottesvolk in Deuteronomium*, Kohlhammer, Stuttgart 1929, and his *Deuteronomium-Studien*, 2nd ed. 1948 (E.T. *Studies in Deuteronomy*); L. Rost, *Die Vorstufe von Kirche und Synagogue im Alten Testament*, Kohlhammer, Stuttgart 1938; N. A. Dahl, *Das Volk Gottes, Eine Untersuchung zum Kirchenbewusstseins des Urchristentums*, Norske Videnskaps Akademi, Oslo 1941. This last book especially, excellently documented, offers a storehouse of data for those who wish to understand the problem of "Church and people" in a Biblical light. I doubt whether H. H. Rowley, *op. cit.*, pp. 86–87, is right if in connection with the "remnant" he voices the thought of "transition from the conception of a nation to that of a Church". Does the Old Testament really know the "conception of a nation"? The constitutive element of Israel is not the common descent (although the call of Abraham, etc., is not wanting), but the act of having been called (qahal) by Yahweh. See, among others, J. D. W. Kritzinger, *Qehal Jahwe, wat dit is en wie daaraan mag behoort* (with a summary in English), J. H. Kok, Kampen 1957. In my opinion it is totally unfruitful in referring to Israel to fasten the word "people" or "nation" on to her apart from her belonging to Yahweh.

26. Vriezen, *op. cit.*, pp. 73 ff.

27. R. B. Y. Scott, *A Kingdom of Priests*, Oudtestamentische Studien VIII, E. J. Brill, Leiden 1950, pp. 213–219. R. Martin-Achard, *Israel et les Nations*, pp. 35–37, concurs with Scott's exegesis.

28. An example of this psychological use of the scheme of particu-

larism and universalism is still found, for example, in A. Amiet, *Origines de la Mission Chrétienne*, in *Le monde non Chrétien*, Paris 1950, p. 860. See further B. Sundkler, *Contributions à l'étude de la pensée missionnaire dans le Nouveau Testament*, Paris 1936. (*Idem, Jésus et les Paiens*, Revue d'Histoire et de Philosophie Religieuses, 1936.)

29. See TWNT I under "hagios". J. Hempel, *Das Ethos des Alten Testaments*, A. Lorentz, Leipzig 1938.

30. L. Rost, *Die Bezeichnungen für Land und Volk*, p. 147; G. Bertram, TWNT II, p. 362.

31. K. L. Schmidt, *Israels Stellung zu den Fremdlingen und Beisassen*, Judaica, Heft I, 1945, p. 284; G. Stählin, TWNT V under "xenos", p. 26; G. Rosen/G. Bertram, *Juden und Phönizier*, 1929. Still of value is the older work of A. Bertholet, *Die Stellung der Israeliten und der Juden zu den Fremden*, J. C. B. Mohr, Tübingen 1896.

32. A clear description of the mutual differences *and* the fundamental agreement in the prophets in his regard is given by M. Schmidt, *Prophet und Tempel, Eine Studie zum Problem der Gottesnähe im Alten Testament*, Zollikon Verlag, Zürich 1948.

33. In a contribution which M. Buber has given to a collective Dutch work on religions of the world, *Godsdiensten der Wereld* (edited by G. v. d. Leeuw, H. Meulenhoff, Amsterdam, 3rd ed. 1954) on "The Faith of Israel", he emphasizes the fact that Exod. 3: 14 must be understood not in an ontological but in an historical sense. It is not a question of the being of God, but a question of God's being present; I am (shall be) who I am (shall be) =I am *there*, and I shall be there, as I shall be.

34. M. Schmidt, *op. cit.*, p. 67.

35. For the rest, the traditional distinction between the historical and the prophetic books in the Old Testament is not without objection. The historical books have to do with a prophetic view of history; the prophetic books with prophecy concerning history. This is emphasized by G. von Rad, *Theologie des Alten Testaments*, I (see note 6 above), and by K. Barth, *Kirchliche Dogmatik*, IV, 3, 1 Hälfte, pp. 58–59 (Zollikon Verlag, Zürich; E.T. *Church Dogmatics*).

36. The only exception to this might perhaps be the well-known passage, Mal. 1: 11. The meaning of this verse must not, however, be given too much weight. The intent of this oft-disputed passage is first and foremost to accentuate the faithlessness of Israel: compared with Israel, the heathen are upright worshippers of Yahweh. We must, therefore, be cautious about any declaration of the positive meaning. Here I differ from the opinion of H. H. Rowley, *The Missionary Message of the Old Testament*: "Perhaps the extreme of broadmindedness found in the Old Testament is found in Malachi" (p. 72); "men who are accepted by God because they have lived up to the light they

had" (p. 74). But an undervaluation of this text, I think, is to be seen in confining it to proselytes and to Jews of the Dispersion. Cf. also R. Martin-Achard, *Israel et les nations*, p. 41: "Malachi is not here pronouncing any absolute judgment on the pagan cult; he is condemning the attitude of the Levites." I believe this can be our reaction: a risky prophetic exclamation which, however, in the light of Israel's attitude and of the promises of salvation to the nations, is not *too* risky. But it is plain that no theory of general revelation or of general grace can be built on this passage.

37. The literature on eschatology in the Old Testament is most extensive. We may cite here, from the older literature, H. Gressmann, *Der Ursprung der Israelitisch-jüdischen Eschatologie*, 1905; *Der Messias*, Vandenhoeck, Göttingen 1929; L. Dürr, *Ursprung und Ausbau der jüdischen Heilandserwartung*, C. A. Schwetschke, Berlin 1925. More recent literature: L. Cerny, *The Day of Jahweh and Some Relevant Problems*, Filosoficke Fakulta Univ. Karlovy, Prague 1948; H. H. Rowley, *The Relevance of Apocalyptic*, 4, Lutterworth Press, London 1952; M. Schmidt, *Prophet und Tempel*, Zollikon Verlag, Zürich 1948; etc. Consult also the literature (just as extensive) on Deutero-Isaiah and the Servant of the Lord. We shall cite only: O. Eissfeldt, *Der Gottesknecht bei Deutero Jesaja*, etc., Halle (Saale) 1933; J. Begrich, *Studien zu Deuterojesaja, Beiträge zur Wissenschaft vom A. und N.T.*, 4 Folge, Heft 25, 1938; J. v. d. Ploeg, *Les chants du Serviteur de Jahvé dans la seconde partie du livre d'Isaïe*, Librairie Lecoffre, Paris 1936; and C. R. North, *The Suffering Servant in Deutero-Isaiah*, Oxford Univ. Press, 1948 (this work gives an extensive bibliography); H. H. Rowley, *The Servant of the Lord*, Lutterworth Press, London 1952; etc.

38. On the Messianic expectation in the Old Testament, a monograph appeared in the Netherlands in 1941 from the hand of A. H. Edelkoort: *De Christusverwachting in het Oude Testament*, H. Veenman, Wageningen. Further, F. E. König, *Messianische Weissagungen*, C. Belser Verlag, Stuttgart 1925; H. Gressmann, *Der Messias*, 1929; H. W. Wolff, *Herrschaft Jahwes und Messiasgestalt im Alten Testament*, ZAW, 1936; W. Vischer, *Das Christuszeugnis des Alten Testaments*, I–III, Zollikon Verlag, Zürich 1934– (E.T. vol. I, *The Witness of the Old Testament to Christ*); M. Buber, *Das Königtum Gottes*, B. Schocken Verlag, 1932; K. Barth, *Kirchliche Dogmatik*, IV, 3, 1 Hälfte, p. 60; see also pp. 61–65 and (2 Hälfte) pp. 788–792. (E.T. *Church Dogmatics*.)

Chapter 2

1. So, e.g., E. Riehm, *Der Missionsgedanke im Alten Testament*, AMZ, 1880; M. Löhr, *Der Missionsgedanke im Alten Testament*, 1896;

A. Bertholet, *Die Stellung der Israeliten und der Juden zu den Fremden*, J. C. B. Mohr, Tübingen 1896. Further, F. M. Th. Böhl, *Oud-Israël en de Zending*; Mededeelingen, Tijdschrift voor Zendingswetenschap, 1929. Otherwise the distinction between universal and missionary is not always kept clear; M. Löhr, *op. cit.*, p. 2, neglects it entirely.

2. Thus, e.g., E. Sellin, *Der Missionsgedanke im Alten Testament*, NAMZ, 1925. So also H. H. Rowley, *The Missionary Message of the Old Testament*, 1944, pp. 9–27, although, in regard to Moses' monotheism, he does say, "For whether Moses regarded other gods as real or not, he certainly regarded them as negligible," p. 21, and later: "it is improbable that Moses attained full monotheism," p. 27.

3. So also Rowley, *op. cit.*: "The man who was the first missionary known to History," p. 27.

4. Cf. H. H. Rowley, *The Faith of Israel*, 1956, p. 185: "With him (Deutero-Isaiah) universalism was the corollary of monotheism and the world-wide mission of Israel the corollary of her election."

5. E. Sellin, *op. cit.*, p. 70; H. H. Rowley, *Missionary Message*, pp. 46–64; E. Jacob, *Théologie de l'Ancien Testament*, 1956, pp. 177–179 (see note 2, Chapter 1 above).

6. So Th. C. Vriezen, *Die Erwählung Israels*, 1953, pp. 62–72, and also H. H. Rowley, *The Biblical Doctrine of Election*; Th. C. Vriezen, *De Zending in het Oude Testament*, De Heerbaan, 1954, pp. 98–110. Further see: J. Blauw, *Goden en Mensen*, 1950, pp. 46–57; M. Schmidt, *Prophet und Tempel*, 1948, pp. 172–191; 221–229.

7. There is too much literature on Deutero-Isaiah and the Servant of the Lord to be listed here. C. R. North, *The Suffering Servant in Deutero-Isaiah*, 1948, gives a good bibliography. Of more recent literature we will cite only: N. H. Snaith, *The Servant of the Lord in Deutero-Isaiah* in *Studies in Old Testament Prophecy* (to Th. H. Robinson,) Ed. Clark, Edinburgh 1950; H. H. Rowley, *The Servant of the Lord*, etc., Lutterworth Press, London 1952; P. A. H. de Boer, *Second Isaiah's Message*, Oudtestamentische Studien XI, 1956; R. Martin-Achard, *Israel et les nations*, Delachaux & Niestlé, Neuchâtel & Paris, 1959.

8. So Vriezen, *op. cit.*, p. 67.

9. *Op. cit.*, Chapter II, pp. 13–30, and especially 23–29.

10. *Op. cit.*, p. 30.

11. Besides the commentaries, introduction and theologies of the Old Testament, see among others, H. H. Rowley, *The Biblical Doctrine of Election*, pp. 67, 86; *The Missionary Message of the Old Testament*, p. 67.

12. H. H. Rowley, *The Faith of Israel*, p. 186.

13. The statement by H. Schmidt, *Die grossen Propheten*, 2nd ed., pp. 483–487 (Van den Hoeck, Göttingen 1923) remains a remarkable one; in this citation he elaborates the opinion he stated as early as

1906 (*Absicht und Entstehungszeit des Buches Jona*, Theol. Studien und Kritiken, 1906, pp. 180–199): Jonah is a polemic against the false prophets; Nineveh is a figure for Jerusalem; if even a godless pagan city is spared, how much more, then, Jerusalem?

14. *Op. cit.*, pp. 45–47. The opinion of A. Feuillet is found in Revue Biblique 54, Paris, Rome 1957, *Le sense du livre de Jonas*, pp. 340–361.

15. Almost every theology of the Old Testament gives a treatment of the characteristic contrast in the Old Testament between nature and history, between naturalism and *Heilsgeschichte*.

16. So the outlook of R. Bultmann regarding the Old Testament. It is the history of the failure of God's covenant with Israel; the failure was unavoidable, because a people of God like Israel is not a real quantity, nor can it be, but only an eschatological one. The sense of the Old Testament is the manifestation of this failure. This conception of Bultmann is closely connected with his eschatological outlook on the New Testament. See R. Bultmann, *Weissagung und Erfüllung*, Zeitschrift für Theologie und Kirche, 1950, pp. 360 ff.

17. W. Vischer, *Das Christuszeugnis des Alten Testaments*, II, 1941, p. 8; K. Barth, *Kirchliche Dogmatik*, IV, 3, p. 792.

18. See G. von Rad, *Theologie des Alten Testaments*, I, pp. 414–415. For the significance of the *chokma*, see Chapter 4, 3.

19. E. Sellin, *Der Missionsgedanke im Alten Testament*, pp. 68–72; P. Volz, *Jesaja II* (Komm. z. A. T.), p. 169, A. Deicherischen Verlagsbuchhandlung, Leipzig; W. Eichrodt, *Gottes Volk und die Völker*, EMM, 1942, Chapter 3; Th. C. Vriezen, *Die Erwählung Israels*, p. 65; H. H. Rowley, *The Missionary Message of the Old Testament*, pp. 46–64; E. Jacob, *Théologie de l'Ancien Testament*, p. 179.

20. P. A. H. de Boer, *Second Isaiah's Message*, Oudtestamentische Studien, XI, 1956, p. 90; N. H. Snaith, *The Servant of the Lord in Deutero-Isaiah*, in *Studies in Old Testament Prophecy*, p. 191; R. Martin-Achard, *Israel et les nations*, pp. 21–30.

21. Particularly Snaith, *op. cit.*, p. 191: "We find . . . this prophet to be essentially nationalistic in attitude. He is actually responsible for the narrow and exclusive attitude of post-exilic days. The so-called Universalism of Deutero-Isaiah needs considerable qualification." It seems to me that Snaith, in his reaction against the *missionary* exegesis and against a one-sided emphasis on the universalistic character of Deutero-Isaiah, goes however too far. For example, when he explains the waiting of the nations in Isa. 42: 4, as a waiting in *fear*, then he concedes that he is going against the ordinary meaning of the Hebrew word; he must appeal to the "Syriac root" of the word to support his thesis!—*op. cit.*, pp. 193–194. In 42: 6, he eliminates "light to the nations" as a gloss, p. 194. In 49: 6, he keeps "light to the nations" but he interprets it as follows: the Servant will be a

light to guide every Israelite wanderer home, p. 198, etc. In the same way the strong item of evidence against Snaith's thesis, in 45: 22, is treated thus—"verse 22 refers to all the scattered Israelites amongst the heathen everywhere," p. 197.

22. One thinks here, for example, of Luke 2: 32, "a light for revelation to the Gentiles," an expression strongly reminiscent of Deutero-Isaiah; likewise Phil. 2: 10–11, etc. Of course it can be said that the New Testament interpretation of Old Testament passages has distorted their original intention. But one might reply that the passages in the New Testament regarding the Old Testament contain the oldest interpretations we have, and on that account commend themselves *a priori*.

23. B. Sundkler, *Jésus et les Païens*, Revue d'Histoire et de Philosophie Religieuses, 1936, pp. 462–499. See also M. Schmidt, *Prophet und Tempel*, 1948, passim. My objection to Sundkler's idea is that he puts too much stress, I believe, on the Temple and the mount of the Temple as the centre, as the "navel of the earth". I believe it would have been sufficient to name Israel here, because, with a few exceptions, such as Ezekiel, the Temple does not play the role in the prophets which Sundkler ascribes to it. But Sundkler is quite right in what he says at the end of his article about the problem of Jesus and the Gentiles (and this goes also, *mutatis mutandis*, for the problem of mission in the Old Testament)—"Only the centripetal interpretation furnishes us with the possibility of a solution to the problem of Jesus and the Gentiles." *Op. cit.*, p. 499.

24. R. Martin-Achard, *op. cit.*, p. 48.

25. *Ibid.*, pp. 71–72.

Chapter 3

1. See, for example, what a relatively slight place Messianism receives in the theologies of the Old Testament of Eichrodt, Köhler, Procksch, von Rad, and Vriezen.

2. One thinks here of the resistance which arose against the Christocentric exegesis of the first chapters of Genesis, for example, by K. Barth, *Kirchliche Dogmatik* III; and especially of the often sharp criticism which has been levelled on the European continent against the work (which is indeed quite controversial) of W. Vischer, *Das Christuszeugnis des Alten Testaments*, 1935–1942. See G. von Rad, *Das Christuszeugnis des Alten Testaments*, Theologische Blätter, 1935; W. Eichrodt, *Zur Frage der theologischen Exegese des Alten Testaments*, Theologische Blätter, 1938; A. H. Edelkoort, *De Christusverwachting in het Oude Testament*, 1941; N. W. Porteous, *Towards a Theology of the Old Testament*, Scottish Journal of Theology, 1948, etc.

3. So, for example, G. Hölscher, *Die Ursprünge der jüdischen Eschatologie*, 1925. One fact which tells against this theory has been pointed out by the majority of critics: the Messiah is rarely designated "King", mostly as "Ruler". Is this to avoid too great a similarity or identification with Israel's kings or with the non-Israelite gods who were called "kings"? (Cf. TWNT I, pp. 563 ff.)

4. This is pointed out by Edelkoort, *op. cit.*, p. 13, where there is a reference to J. Brierre Marbonne, *Les prophètes messianiques de l'Ancien Testament dans la littérature juive*, Paul Geuthner Librairie Orientaliste, Paris 1933.

5. Cf. TWNT I, p. 565.

6. This is emphatically stated by H. H. Rowley, *The Unity of the Bible*, Carey Kingsgate Press, London 1953. In the recent little book by G. von Rad, *Moses*, World Christian Books, no. 32, Lutterworth Press, London 1960, there is visible this synthesis *after* the analysis; likewise, of course, in his *Theologie des Alten Testaments*. Highly important are von Rad's expositions in Vol. II, pp. 329–424 (1960. E.T. in preparation).

7. See here the important exposition by K. Barth, *Kirchliche Dogmatik*, IV, 3, 1 Hälfte, pp. 52–78.

8. Cf. H. Gressmann, *Der Messias*, pp. 472 ff.

9. So G. von Rad in TWNT I, p. 565, "basileus".

10. Though the Messianic exegesis of Gen. 3: 15 has been abandoned in many circles, and even quite strongly contested, I think it is not out of line to remark that an early Messianic note is indeed struck here in the promise of the destruction of the serpent (if this is understood as an anti-godly power). In any case, Gen. 3: 15 must be read as a promise of something to be enacted in the future history of man. Gen. 3 must also be read as a confession of the *Geschichtsmächtigkeit* (power in history) of the God of Israel. In the light of the New Testament fulfilment, this passage certainly takes on Messianic significance.

11. The Messianic significance of the priesthood in Israel must be interpreted negatively; the *impotence* of the priestly sacrifice, the limits of priestly service are more Messianic than the priesthood itself. The impotence of the priestly sacrifice really to effect forgiveness "keeps the wound open". Cf. TWNT III, "archiereus," p. 278.

12. Against Edelkoort, *op. cit.*, p. 76, and others, it is my intention to hold fast to the Messianic exegesis of this passage. Cf. also G. von Rad, *Moses*, p. 78.

13. So H. W. Wolff, *Herrschaft Jahwehs*, p. 174; Vriezen, *Theologie*, p. 239; Gressmann, *Messias*, p. 271; von Rad, TWNT I, pp. 563 ff.; and others.

14. Von Rad, TWNT I, p. 566, note: "The Servant of the Lord songs in Deutero-Isaiah do not refer to the Messiah." There is no

147

need here for us to discuss the point. The literature is indicated in note 37, Chapter I, and further in the summary in TWNT V, pp. 653–654.

15. In all likelihood the Servant of the Lord was interpreted Messianically even in pre-Christian times. For this, see among others, J. Héring, *Le royaume de Dieu et sa venue*, Delachaux & Niestlé, Neuchâtel & Paris, 1937, p. 67; C. W. North, *The Suffering Servant*, p. 7. See also TWNT V, pp. 685 ff.

16. Zimmerli, TWNT V, p. 669.

17. On the significance of the remnant—an important Old Testament item into which we have not been able to enter because of shortness of space—H. H. Rowley has written in *The Biblical Doctrine of Election*, 3rd ed. 1953, pp. 69–94. We object to his remark on pp. 86–87: "Not all Israel was elect, and not all the elect were of Israel. There was thus the transition from the conception of a nation to that of a Church, from the thought of a body of people held together by their common descent to that of a people held together by a common faith." For it does not seem right to me to call Israel a "nation with a common descent". It is the election that prohibits *any* emphasis on this element; from the very beginning Israel is "a people held together by a common faith". It seems to me a shifting of the Biblical witness to compare the relationship of Israel and the remnant to that of nation and Church. I think one might have to speak of a faithful and unfaithful people of God, an unfaithful people and a remnant *made* faithful. This is not to deny that Israel has not known the tension of "nation and Church", but it is to deny that the Old Testament recognizes any Church-people opposition as we understand it (with the background of the history of our national Churches). See also TWNT IV, pp. 148–173 under "eklegomai" (Quell); O. Cullmann, *Christus und die Zeit*, Zollikon Verlag, Zürich 1946, pp. 99 ff. (E.T. *Christ and Time*).

18. J. Jeremias, TWNT VI, p. 537, points out that "many" occurs five times, so that this word becomes a characteristic of this passage of Scripture.

19. In the light of the Messianic appropriation of the Servant of the Lord songs, I am inclined to approve of R. Martin-Achard in his exegesis of Isa. 42:4: The nations shall look upon the work that God has done to Israel. So *Israel et les nations*, p. 26. Apart from that, Martin-Achard, like many recent exegetes (P.A.H. de Boer, N. H. Snaith, and others) ignores the Messianic character of the songs.

20. I pass by the question as to an individual or collective conception of the Son of Man (in connection with Dan. 7:27). For this see F. E. König, *Messianische Weissagungen*, 3rd ed., 1925, p. 309; Edelkoort, *Christusverwachting*, pp. 497 ff., and the commentaries.

Personally, I believe that we must take account here of a certain fluidity, just as we must in the figure of the Servant in Deutero-Isaiah. Furthermore, the representative function of both the Servant of the Lord and of the Son of Man forms a link between the individual and the collective "poles". This conception renders superfluous the forced solution of the difficulties in Dan. 7 as presented by Edelkoort (*op. cit.*, p. 500—non-Messianic elaboration of originally Messianic material). See also G. von Rad, *Theologie des A.T.* II, pp. 264-274.

21. H. Gressmann, *Der Messias*, pp. 344 ff.

22. There is a remarkable exegesis from the hand of the Jewish exegete M. Buber regarding the matter of the bearing of sin in Isa. 53; this is found in *Het Geloof van Israël* (The Faith of Israel) in the Dutch symposium edited by G. v. d. Leeuw, *De Godsdiensten der Wereld*, 2nd ed., 1948, p. 300. According to Buber, this sin cannot refer to the transgressions of Israel, for these are borne by God Himself. Buber refers to Hos. 14: 3, Jer. 33: 24. The gods of the nations do not do this; the gods bow under the load, but they cannot carry it. (So Buber explains Isa. 46: 2.) Now the Servant of the Lord will do what the gods cannot do, namely, bear the ills and the painful evil of the sins of the nations, Isa. 53: 4. "My people", then, in Isa. 53: 8, is put in the mouth of each of the kings who, as it appears from Isa. 52: 13-15, is on his feet. Although this exegesis appears to me forced and untenable, it certainly has this much truth—that the bearing of sin also includes those of the nations. In this respect the exegesis of *this* son of Israel is an unsuspected witness for the Old Testament preaching of the world-redeeming power of Messianic suffering (even though Buber himself conceives of the Servant of the Lord not as personally Messianic, but as collectively or individually Israelite).

23. The contrast existing here with the older directly missionary exegesis is not so irreconcilable as it perhaps seems at first glance. We are much further along, I believe, when we can come to the following *communis opinio* in regard to the Old Testament:

(a) There is no explicit, but only at best an implicit indication of mission in the centrifugal sense. The idea of mission can in consequence only be *derived* (at best) from the eschatological and Messianic passages and is never to be *read* directly.

(b) Mission as an *act* of *men* lies quite outside the Old Testament circle of concern.

(c) Only in the liturgy of Israel (the Psalms) does Israel rise, as it were, above herself and call the nations to universal praise, which still, however, finds its inspiration in the acts of God in and with Israel.

24. For this, see TWNT II, pp. 400-405, under "eirene"; J. C. Hoekendijk, *The Call to Evangelism*, IRM, 1950, pp. 162-175.

1. Of the earlier literature (before 1930) on this subject I only mention (in chronological order):

A. Bertholet, *Die Stellung der Israeliten und der Juden zu den Fremden*, 1896.

K. Axenfeld, *Die jüdische Propaganda als Vorläuferin und Wegbereiterin der urchristlichen Mission. Festschrift für G. Warneck*, 1904.

P. Wendland, *Die hellenistisch-römische Kultur in ihren Beziehungen zu Judentum und Christentum*, 2. Aufl. J. C. B. Mohr, Tübingen 1912.

A. Causse, *La propaganda juive et l'hellenisme*, Revue d'Histoire et de Philosophie religieuses, II, 1923.

W. Bousset, *Die Religion des Judentums im späthellenistischen Zeitalter*, 3. Aufl. J. C. B. Mohr, Tübingen 1926.

A. Causse, *Les dispersés d'Israel*. Etudes Strassbourg 19, Paris 1929.

G. Rosen, *Das antike Judentum als Missionsreligion und die Entstehung der jüdischen Diaspora*. Neu bearbeitet und erweitert von Fr. Rosen und G. Bertram. Tübingen 1929;

and of the literature from 1930 onwards:

F. M. Derwacter, *Preparing the Way for Paul, The Proselyte Movement in later Judaism*. The Macmillan Company, New York 1930.

A. Causse, *Le judaisme avant Jésus Christ*. Paris 1931.

Paul Volz, Fr. Stummer, Joh. Hempel (Herausgeber), *Werden und Wesen des A.T.: Vorträge gehalten auf der internationalen Tagung a.t. licher Forscher zu Göttingen vom 4–10 Sept. 1935*, Alfred Töpelmans, Berlin 1936. In this work especially: A. Causse, *La Sagesse et la propaganda juive à l'époque perse et hellenistique*, pp. 148–154.

B. J. Bamberger, *Proselytism in the Talmudic Period*, Hebrew Union College Press, Cincinnati 1939.

R. H. Charles, *Religious development between the Old and New Testaments*. Oxford Univ. Press, revised ed. 1945.

P. Dalbert, *Die Theologie der hellenistisch-jüdischen Missionsliteratur unter Ausschluss von Philo und Josephus*, Theol. Forschung, Herausgeber H. W. Bartsch IV Herb. Reich, Evang. Verlag Hamburg Volks-dorf 1954.

The works of E. Stauffer are of importance to those who want to understand Judaism at the time of the beginning of the Christian Church in the light of the Qumran literature. Stauffer gives a good and popular survey in: *Jerusalem und Rom im Zeitalter Jesu Christi*, Dalp Taschenbücher Band 331, Francke Verlag, Berne & Munich 1957, with 32 pages of notes.

2. Derwacter, *op. cit.*, p. 119.

3. *Ibid.*, p. 76.

4. Bamberger, *op. cit.*, pp. 17–19.

5. Dalbert, *op. cit.*, p. 22.

6. Derwacter, *op. cit.*, p. 21.

7. G. Rosen, etc., *op. cit.*, p. 25.

8. A. v. Harnack, *Die Mission und Ausbreitung des Christentums in den ersten drei Jahrhunderten.* 4. Aufl. J. C. Hinrichs, Leipzig 1924, p. 12.

9. We refer to the important work of P. Dalbert. We cannot go any further into it.

10. Bamberger in particular resists the accepted idea that the Christian Church dislodged and expelled Jewish missionary effort. He supports his opinion by references to the Halaga and the Haggada.

11. Bamberger, *op. cit.*, pp. 267–273. The words cited are on page 272.

12. P. Dalbert, *op. cit.*, pp. 23–26.

13. G. Bertram in *Juden und Phönizier*, p. 36.

14. *Ibid.*, p. 49.

15. *Ibid.*, p. 141.

16. *Ibid.*, p. 36.

17. *Ibid.*, pp. 49–50.

18. Jewish *Sibylle* III, 195.

19. Horace, *Satires* I, 4, 143. G. Bertram, *op. cit.*, p. 151.

20. P. Dalbert, *op. cit.*, passim, and particularly pp. 124–143.

21. For earlier literature we refer to W. Baumgartner's survey, *Die Israelitische Weisheitsliteratur*, Theologische Rundschau 1933, pp. 259–300; K. Galling, *Stand und Aufgabe der Kohelet Forschung*, Theol. Rundschau 1934; pp. 355–373. See also the notes in R. H. Pfeiffer, *Introduction to the Old Testament*, Harper Bros., New York and London, 1941, pp. 873–875; C. Rylarsdam, *Revelation in Jewish wisdom literature*, 1951; H. J. Kraus, *Die Verkündigung der Weisheit*, Bibl. Studien Heft 2, 1951; G. von Rad, *Theologie des A.T.* I, 1957, pp. 439–451. For general information: see the introductions to the comments on Proverbs.

22. Von Rad, *op. cit.*, p. 442.

23. *Ibid.*, p. 444.

24. This was mainly inspired by Ecclesiasticus 17, and in particular by 17 v. 17 (Septuagint Alfr. Rahlfs ed. Vol. II, p. 405: "He ordered that each nation should have a leader but the Lord inherits Israel").

25. Von Rad, *op. cit.*, p. 449.

26. I thought at first that I would have to restrict myself to the data to be found in the Bible in the survey that the I.M.C. asked me to write. However, during the "European Consultation" on the first draft of my survey, held in Geneva (July 11–14, 1960), I was asked to add something about the period between Old Testament and New Testament and particularly about the wisdom literature. This short chapter was written to comply with that request. I did not have time,

however, to deal extensively with either the diaspora mission or the *chokma* of the Old Testament. In my opinion the brief mention I made of it is sufficient for the purpose for which this survey was written. However, in a study of the relation between revelation and religion ("the Word of God and the living faiths of men") the *chokma* would have to be dealt with in great detail!

§3 has been incorporated in this chapter and not in Chapter 3, in spite of the fact that it, unlike §1 and 2, deals with data from the Bible itself, for the following reasons:

It seems to me that in the present state of the investigation into the *chokma* (c.q. my limited knowledge of this investigation) it cannot very well be decided whether chapters 1–9 of Proverbs should be considered to be (late) post-exile. I think that the nature of the *chokma*, particularly when seen as the starting point and stimulus for apocalyptics and missionary activity after the exile, partly justify §3's being incorporated in this chapter. I hope I may be forgiven this irregularity (from the point of view of composition). In a survey like the present, in which considerations of the history of salvation play an important role, the phenomenon of the almost "a-historic" *chokma* is a healthy counterbalance to a too rectilinear idea of the history of salvation.

27. See the document of the World Council of Churches on proselytism: *Christian Witness, Proselytism and Religious Liberty in the Setting of the World Council of Churches*, 1956.

Chapter 5

1. A survey and discussion of the older conceptions is given by B. Sundkler in *Jésus et les Païens*, Revue d'Histoire et de Philosophie Religieuses, 16, 1936, pp. 462–499, also published in 1937 in *Arbeiten und Mitteilungen aus dem neutestamentlichen Seminar zu Uppsala*, 1937, pp. 1–38.

Because these older conceptions are perhaps still thought to be tenable in certain quarters, we may call some attention to them here.

In the nineteenth century various scholars (Strauss, Weiss, Holzmann, among others) maintained that Jesus gradually came from a particularistic point of view to a conviction of universalism. This evolutionary idea, typical of the nineteenth century, was stigmatized by Gustav Warneck as a fantasy; for this conviction he depended upon the systematic work of M. Kähler.

A. v. Harnack (1906) emphasized the "intensive universalism" of Jesus, though Jesus kept mission beyond His horizon. Against this view F. Spitta (1908) protested, by suggesting that Jesus Himself worked and preached beyond the borders of Israel. Following him the Roman Catholic scholar M. Meinertz (1908) also opposed the "intensive universalism" of Harnack, proposing in its stead "explicit universalism". Meinertz later (1926) clarified his position by suggesting clearly that Jesus willed the mission to the Gentiles.

A. Schweitzer (1930) attacked the problem from a completely different angle, by emphasizing the eschatological character of Jesus' universalism: "Jesus thought universalistically and acted particularistically." B. Sundkler, by contrast, suggests that the solution of the problem can only be found (1) by dropping the false alternative between particularism and universalism; (2) by turning our attention to the eschatological significance of Zion, Jerusalem and especially the Temple as the reintegration centre of the world.

The most important studies on this question which have appeared since Sundkler's essay are the following: N. A. Dahl, *Das Volk Gottes*, Skrifter Utgitt ar det Norske Videnskaps Akademi, Oslo 1941, pp. 143–167; A. G. Hebert, *The Throne of David*, 2nd ed., 1942; H. Stoevesandt, *Jesus und die Heidenmission*, 1943 (of which only a résumé is accessible, in Theologische Literaturzeitung 1949, p. 242); R. Liechtenhan, *Die Urchristliche Mission*, Zwingli Verlag, Zürich 1946; T. W. Manson, *Jesus and the Non-Jews*, Athlone Press, London 1955; and particularly J. Jeremias, *Jesu Verheissung für die Völker*, Kohlhammer Verlag, Stuttgart 1956 (E.T. *Jesus' Promise to the Nations*). The last-named work gives a bibliography in chronological order, which is virtually complete; however, the above-cited works of Sundkler and Jeremias are missing, as is O. Cullman, *Christus und die Zeit*, 1946 (E.T. *Christ and Time*).

Subsequent to the work of Jeremias there appeared: O. Cullmann, *Die Christologie des Neuen Testaments*, J. C. B. Mohr, Tübingen 1957 (E.T. *The Christology of the New Testament*), which opens new approaches to this problem; and H. W. Bartsch, *Die Passions- und Ostergeschichten bei Matthäus* in *Basileia*, 1959 (*W. Freytag zum 60. Geburtstag*), pp. 27–41. The extensive work by H. N. Ridderbos, *De Komst van het Koninkrijk*, J. H. Kok, Kampen 1950, which has since appeared in the U.S.A. under the title *The Coming of the Kingdom* (Presbyterian and Reformed Publ. Cy., Philadelphia 1961) also gives much material.

I think in the main we can now speak of a consensus in missionary circles regarding the problem before us, particularly, I believe, thanks to the writings of Sundkler and Jeremias, which have attracted great attention everywhere.

The observations made in this chapter are inspired in particular by the publications which have appeared since Sundkler's essay in 1936.

2. This is pointed out by Jeremias, *op. cit.*, p. 35.

3. An excellent discussion of these two passages is found in Jeremias, *op. cit.*, pp. 16–22 and pp. 9–16.

4. Jeremias, *op. cit.*, pp. 22–32.

5. J. Hempel, *Der synoptische Jesus und das Alte Testament*, ZAW 1938, pp. 1–33, particularly p. 29: "Jesus has erected no 'national' barriers; He has removed in a lasting manner the basis of the national exclusiveness of Judaism, when it was able to make proselytes, but He has not shattered the historical continuity of revelation."

6. Jeremias, *op. cit.*, pp. 34–39. Jeremias' interpretation of Luke 4: 22 is noteworthy. He sees in this verse the resistance of the Jews against Jesus' preaching of grace for the Gentiles. The inhabitants of Nazareth would have resented it because Jesus had eliminated the thought of *vengeance* from the eschatological expectation (cf. Luke 4: 18 and Isa. 61: 2). He points out the analogy in Matt. 11: 5 ff. (Luke 7: 22 ff.), where the prophetic promises are quoted from Isa. 35: 4 ff., 29: 18 ff., 61: 1–2, *without* a mention of the vengeance of God which is explicitly stated in the Isaiah passages.

In spite of the arguments, I cannot agree in this respect with the study of Jeremias, which in other respects is so excellent. Is it not quite beyond debate that Nazareth objected particularly to the *Messianic* declarations of Jesus ("Is this not Joseph's son?" Luke 4: 22) and thus also to His appropriation of the eschatological promises of salvation? I do not deny that Jesus, in His proclamation of salvation for the Gentiles, was also touching a very raw nationalistic nerve.

7. Jeremias, *op. cit.*, pp. 40–44.

8. H. N. Ridderbos, *Zelfopenbaring en Zelfverberging*, J. H. Kok, Kampen 1950, passim; *De Komst van het Koninkrijk*, 1954, pp. 35–68 (see note 1 above); O. Cullmann, *Die Christologie des Neuen Testaments*, 1957, pp. 138–198 (see note 1 above) where further bibliography is given.

9. For the complex of questions surrounding (Messianic) expectation and fulfilment, see also: W. G. Kümmel, *Verheissung und Erfüllung*, 1945, 2nd ed. 1953; *Untersuchungen zur eschatologischen Verkündigung Jesu* (Abhandlungen zur Theologie des Alten und Neuen Testaments 6), Zwingli Verlag, Zürich. (E.T. *Promise and Fulfilment; the Eschatological Message of Jesus.*)

10. For this see Chapter 6.

11. From the extensive literature about Jesus as the Servant of the Lord only a few recent works are cited here (and in these one can find reference to further literature, particularly older works): E. Lohmeyer, *Gottesknecht und Davidssohn*, Symbolae Biblicae Upsalienses E. Muukogaard, Hafulae, Sweden, 1945, 2nd ed. 1953; H. W. Wolff, *Jesaja 53 im Urchristentum*, Evang. Verlagsanstalt, Berlin, 2nd ed. 1950; M. Buber, *Jesus und der Knecht* in *Pro Regno—Pro Sanctuario*, *Feestbundel G. v. d. Leeuw*, G. F. Callenbach, Nijkerk 1950; J. Jeremias, "Pais Theou" in TWNT V, 1952, pp. 676–713; T. W. Manson, *The*

Servant Messiah, Cambridge Univ. Press, 1953; O. Cullmann, *Die Christologie des Neuen Testaments*, 1957, pp. 50–81 (see note 1 above).

12. So, for example, Liechtenhan (*Urchr. Mission*, p. 40), Ridderbos (*Komst van het Koninkrijk*, p. 328), Jeremias (TWNT V, p. 713, VI, pp. 536–545).

13. See also E. Lohse, *Märtyrer und Gottesknecht*, etc., Vandenhoeck & Rupprecht, Göttingen 1955; J. Jeremias, *Jesu Verheissung für die Völker*, p. 45 (E.T. *Jesus' Promise to the Nations*).

14. *Ibid.*, pp. 45–46.

15. *Ibid.*, pp. 48–53.

16. Doesn't Sundkler lay too much emphasis on the *Temple* as the "navel of the earth"? Though this general oriental image may not have been foreign to Israel, I do not think it right to impute to the Temple so much significance. Outside of Ezekiel, nowhere in the Old Testament do we find the *Temple* called the centre. Jerusalem and Zion, we do. I think this is not without significance in relation to the dying out of the Temple service in Israel in the first century A.D. The criticism of the overemphasis on the Temple which I levelled in my *Goden en Mensen*, 1950, p. 110, I would now make stronger. In the same spirit, see Liechtenhan, *op. cit.*, p. 37.

It occurs to me that Jeremias, *op. cit.*, p. 52, has taken over and underlined Sundkler's centripetal idea, but without his conception of the central and all-important significance of the Temple. He is right in naming the Temple as one of the eschatological images, p. 55.

17. After the example of H. Stoevesandt, *op. cit.*, p. 53.

18. Jeremias, *op. cit.*, p. 54. In this respect his exegesis of John 8: 56 is especially illuminating and, I think, convincing: "When the gospel of John has Jesus say that Abraham rejoiced that he was to see Jesus' day, this *echarē* includes the joy of Abraham over the imminent fulfilment of the promise made to him, that he would be the father of a multitude of nations (Gen. 17: 4, Rom. 4: 17)." For the parables of Jesus see among others H. N. Ridderbos, *De Komst van het Koninkrijk*, pp. 124 ff.; J. Jeremias, *Die Gleichnisse Jesu*, 3rd ed., 1954 (E.T. *The Parables of Jesus*).

19. Jeremias, *Jesu Verheissung*, pp. 54–56.

20. *Ibid.*, pp. 57–58.

21. *Ibid.*, p. 59.

22. K. Barth, *Kirchliche Dogmatik*, IV, 3, p. 1047.

23. J. Jeremias, *op. cit.*, pp. 60–62; H. N. Ridderbos, *De Komst van het Koninkrijk*, pp. 161–166; V. Taylor, *Jesus and His Sacrifice*, Macmillan, London 1948, pp. 82–200.

24. In this I am thinking of the school of the so-called consistent or radical eschatology, which has emerged since Joh. Weiss published his *Die Predigt vom Reiche Gottes* in 1892 and which has received the

greatest attention through the work of A. Schweitzer, *Die Geschichte der Leben Jesu Forschung*, 1906, 4th ed. with another title, 1933 (E.T. *The Quest of the Historical Jesus*), and in modified form by M. Dibelius, and in even tighter form by R. Bultmann, C. H. Dodd, and others. Criticism and reaction to this point of view may be found (with a strong emphasis on the *heilsgeschichtliche* character of the gospels) in J. Jeremias, E. Stauffer, W. G. Kümmel, O. Cullmann, T. W. Manson, and others. See among others F. Buri, *Die Bedeutung der neutestamentlichen Eschatologie für die neuere protestantische Theologie*, Feldegg A. G., Zürich 1934; H. D. Wendland, *Die Eschatologie des Reiches Gottes bei Jesus*, Bertelsmann, Gütersloh 1931; O. Cullmann, *Christus und die Zeit*, 1946, etc. H. N. Ridderbos, *De Komst van het Koninkrijk*, 1950, p. 62, points out that detracting from the idea of vicarious suffering is one of the ultimate causes of the foreshortening of the New Testament perspective in the so-called consistent eschatology.

See E. Stauffer, *Jerusalem und Rom im Zeitalter Jesu Christi*, Dalp Taschenbücher 331, Francke Verlag, Berne & Munich 1960, p. 7; also Chapter 7 in the same book, "Die jüdische Naherwartung", pp. 74–87 and 145–147.

25. There is no theological distinction between the designations "Kingdom of God", "Kingdom of Heaven", "Kingdom of the Father", "Kingdom of Christ". We must view various earlier attempts to discover a real theological difference as a failure, and almost all of these attempts have now been given up. See TWNT I, "basileia", p. 582. Further H. D. Wendland, *Die Eschatologie des Reiches Gottes bei Jesus*, Bertelsmann, Gütersloh 1931; H. M. Matter, *Nieuwere Opvattingen omtrent het Koninkrijk Gods in Jezus' Prediking naar de Synoptici*, J. H. Kok, Kampen 1942; and also the various theologies of the New Testament.

26. See, for example, Mark 1 : 14, 15.

27. We take our stand once more against the views of R. Bultmann, C. H. Dodd, and others, who will not recognize a new expectation in *historical perspective*. Here we cannot go into the whole discussion around the consistent, radical, or "realized" eschatology. For this, see, for example, W. G. Kümmel, *Verheissung und Erfüllung*, 1945; O. Cullmann, *Christus und die Zeit*, 1946; H. N. Ridderbos, *De Komst van het Koninkrijk*, 1950.

It is impossible, I believe, to obtain a correct view of the purport and range of the call to mission when we take the standpoint of radical eschatology. I think this is an abridgment of the *heilsgeschichtlich* perspective and, what is worse, in fact a denial of it. An attempt to build a science of missions and of religions from a kerygma understood "existentially" was made by W. Holsten in his *Das Kerygma und der Mensch*, Ch. Kaiser Verlag, Munich 1958.

28. The problem of the Second Coming, expected in the near future, and of disappointment over its delay, has influenced and sometimes controlled discussion concerning the synoptic gospels for the last several decades. This discussion, which also carries great importance for the theory of mission, does not yet seem to have reached a conclusion.

For a survey of earlier literature in this regard see F. Busch, *Zum Verständnis der synoptischen Eschatologie, Markus 13 neu untersucht*, Bertelsmann, Gütersloh 1938. For more recent studies see the works cited in note 27 above. A short survey of the various newer theories is given by Ridderbos, *op. cit.*, pp. 372–383.

29. So, for example, O. Cullmann, *op. cit.*, p. 75. "Intensity [that is, of expectation for the future (Blauw)] and central position, however, are not to be confused." (American edition, Westminster Press, 1950, p. 86.) Likewise pp. 77–78: "In the light of this Primitive Christian outlook, the entire complex of questions concerning the expectation of the imminent end and the delay of the Parousia has lost its importance in interim Christianity." (American edition, pp. 89–90.)

30. This conception becomes visible in K. Barth's *Auslegung von Matth. 28: 16–20*, Basler Missionsbuchhandlung, Basel 1945, pp. 5–6. But later Barth has given evidence of a much more subtle, and, I think, more acceptable conception, viz. in *Kirchliche Dogmatik* IV, 3, 1 Hälfte, pp. 341–342, where he speaks about three forms, appearances, or stages of the one occurrence of Christ's Second Coming, which none the less form a unity and which must be imagined as a sort of perichoresis. He concludes his remarks carefully: "Plainly not all locks are to be opened with this key. But it would be advisable not to disdain this one alongside others," p. 342.

In the matter of the connection between resurrection and Parousia, the view of H. W. Bartsch is probably the most pronounced. But see his contribution in *Basileia* (*W. Freytag zum 60. Geburtstag*), Evang. Missionsverlag, Stuttgart 1959, pp. 27–41, where, I think, he softens his earlier statements himself when he ends: "The Parousia has already happened and yet is awaited at the same time with every manifestation of His lordship." *Op. cit.*, p. 41. J. Jeremias also sees a very close connection between resurrection and Parousia and wishes in this way to solve the problem of the expectation for the near future. See his contribution *Eine neue Schau der Zukunftsaussagen Jesu* in Theologische Blätter, 1941, pp. 217–222.

31. Here, I think, there is an element of truth which will stand, which the defenders of radical eschatology have brought out clearly, when their starting-point is the assumption that the Kingdom of God *had* come in Jesus; but it is this assumption which is not generally

recognized. Eschatology is destined to remain eschatology unto all generations. By this means violence is done to the *historical* character of the revelation of God, and this is exchanged for an *idealistic* interpretation. The explanation of the fact that Jeremias, Bartsch, and others view the Second Coming of Christ (as the end of days) as already completed in the resurrection of Christ, lies, it seems to me, in their acceptance of the character of *fulfilment* of the gospels. From this point of departure, however, which in itself is correct, a mistaken conclusion has been drawn, I believe.

32. This has been emphasized particularly by O. Cullmann: "Unless we make the necessary limitation, it is false to assert that Primitive Christianity had an eschatological orientation. That is true only of Judaism. On the contrary, even for Jesus, while He is dwelling upon earth, it no longer is true in the Jewish sense. The norm is no longer that which is to come; it is He who has already come. Eschatology is not put aside, but it is dethroned, and this holds good both chronologically and essentially. The stripping away of eschatology, when understood in the sense just indicated, is nevertheless linked with a heightened intensity of expectation for the future: this stripping away coincides with the appearance of Christ, and is conditioned by this positive fact rather than by delay of the Parousia." *Op. cit.*, pp. 122–123. (American edition, p. 139.)

33. No justice, I think, is done to this prevailing or new expectation for the future when so much weight is given to the *heilsgeschichtliche* fulfilment that the expectation grows pale or is hollow. I do not think Cullmann, *op. cit.*, entirely avoids this danger. When he says (see note 32): "the norm is no longer that which is to come; it is He who has already come," this is correct only when we add, "*and* He who shall come again!"

The maintenance and underlining of the *future* element in the preaching of the Kingdom of heaven and in the expectation of the Church is also argued for by H. N. Ridderbos, *op. cit.*, pp. 51–60, 361–443.

34. Ridderbos, *op. cit.*, p. 124. In this passage he cites Bengel's *Gnomon, parabola de semina prima ac fundamentalis.*

35. *Ibid.*, p. 125.

36. Schniewind, *Markus*, p. 73, quoted in Ridderbos, *op. cit.*, p. 126. For other explanations of this parable, see *op. cit.*, pp. 127–129.

37. *Ibid.*, p. 132.

38. *Ibid.*, pp. 134–135.

39. *Ibid.*, p. 135.

40. *Ibid.*, p. 141.

41. O. Cullmann, *op. cit.*, pp. 96–97.

42. Another evidence that great significance must be attached to

this judgment as a characteristic and portion of the Messianic self-revelation is found in Matt. 3: 12; for John the Baptist, the day of the Messiah is the day of judgment. Thence comes his confusion, Matt. 11: 2-3. It is important here also to note that Jesus eliminates judgment from the prophetic expectation in His preaching in Nazareth; cf. J. Jeremias, *Jesu Verheissung für die Völker*, pp. 35-39.

43. O. Cullmann, *op. cit.*, p. 122; cf. note 32 above.

44. On the functioning of eschatology and the resistance against it in mission circles, see H. J. Margull, *Theologie der missionarischen Verkündigung, Evangelisation als Oekumenisches Problem*, Evang. Verlagswerk, Stuttgart 1959, pp. 24-38.

45. On the place and function of the apostles in general: K. H. Rengstorf in TWNT I, 1933, "apostolos", pp. 406-448. A survey of the literature up to 1930 may be found here, p. 406; literature from 1930-50 may be found in the survey by H. Mosbeck, *Apostolos in the New Testament* (Studia Theologica 1949-50, pp. 167-200). For the literature after 1950 see, among others, O. Cullmann, *Petrus, Jünger, Apostel, Märtyrer*, Zwingli Verlag, Zürich 1952 (E. T. *Peter: Disciple, Apostle, Martyr*); E. Lohse, *Ursprung und Prägung des christlichen Apostolates*, Theol. Zeitschrift, 1953. In Holland, since 1950: A. A. van Ruler, *Bijzonder en algemeen ambt*, G. F. Callenbach, Nijkerk 1952; H. N. Ridderbos, *De apostoliciteit der kerk volgens het Nieuwe Testament*, in: *De Apostolische Kerk*, J. H. Kok, Kampen 1954, pp. 39-97.

46. Rengstorf, *op. cit.*, pp. 415-418, and also p. 421: "The Greek furnishes therefore only the form of the New Testament concept; the content is determined by the *šālîah* of late Judaism." H. Dürr also turns against the employment of the concept of apostolate for mission, *Kirche, Mission und Reich Gottes*, EMM, September 1953, pp. 133-145.

47. Cf., for example, Acts 14: 4, where Paul and Barnabas are also called apostles.

48. O. Cullmann, *Petrus*, p. 219.

49. Ridderbos, *Apost. Kerk*, pp. 54-55.

50. It seems unjust to me to apply the Old Testament idea of the remnant to the apostles: (1) because this remnant is represented rather by Jesus Himself—the remnant who is a substitute for the whole people; (2) because the apostles certainly occupy a unique position in the early Christian Church as witnesses and founders, but never, as far as I can see, a substituting one; (3) because in all the continuity with the Old Testament, the new thing about the apostles is the fact that they are just as much the beginning of a new people as they are the continuation of the old people. Therefore the miracle of the Church cannot be understood if the fact of Israel's election is not understood. For this, see N. A. Dahl, *Das Volk Gottes*, 1941, passim.

51. O. Michel, *Menschensohn und Völkerwelt*, EMZ, 1941, p. 266.

52. It might be useful to note that wherever in this chapter the word Church has been used, this refers exclusively to the ecclesia as the community of the Kingdom as it occurs in the Gospels and not to the Church in an institutional or even in a denominational sense. One of the greatest and haughtiest heresies in the history of the Church is the identification of the institution with this community of the Kingdom. A healthy ecclesiology does not identify these two but lets the institutional Church be supplied with norms time and time again by the N.T. community of the Kingdom. If the expectation of and the direction towards the Kingdom should become the criterion for the Church as an institution and denomination, there might be quite a smaller number of "true" and "false" churches, and the idea of "sect" might be handled with less assurance.

53. H. Dürr, *op. cit.*, p. 141.

Chapter 6

1. For the whole of the revelation of God in regard to Israel and the nations see also: K. Barth, *Kirchliche Dogmatik* IV, 3, 1 Hälfte, pp. 54–67, 2 Hälfte, pp. 788–792.

2. For this section in general, see: O. Michel, *Gottesherrschaft und Völkerwelt*, EMZ 1941, pp. 225–232; *Menschensohn und Völkerwelt*, EMZ, 1941, pp. 257–267; *Gemeinde und Völkerwelt*, EMZ, 1941, pp. 289–295; *Der Heilige Geist in der Völkerwelt*, EMZ, 1941, pp. 321–328; *Die Fürbitte des Erlösers*, EMZ, 1941, pp.353–360; W. Freytag, *Mission im Blick aufs Ende*, EMZ, 1942, pp. 321–328; K. Barth, *Auslegung von Matth. 28: 16–20*, 1945; R. Liechtenhan, *Die Urchristliche Mission*, 1946; H. H. Rowley, *The Relevance of Apocalyptic*, 1947; J. Blauw, *Goden en Mensen*, 1950; G. Stählin, *Die Endschau Jesu und die Mission*, EMZ, 1950, pp. 97–105, 134–147; O. Michel, *Der Abschluss des Matthäusevangeliums*, Evangelische Theologie 10, 1950–51, pp. 16–26; E. Lohmeyer, *Mir ist gegeben alle Gewalt, Eine Exegese von Matth. 28: 16–20*, in *In memoriam E. Lohmeyer* 1951, pp. 22–49; J. Marsh, *The Fullness of Time*, 1952; P. S. Minear, *Christian Hope and the Second Coming*, 1953; J. E. Fison, *The Christian Hope, the Presence and the Parousia*, Longmans, London 1954; S. Knak, *Neutestamentliche Missionstexte nach neuerer Exegese*, Theologia Viatorum V, 1954, pp. 27–50; K. G. Kuhn, *Das Problem der Mission in der Urchristenheit*, EMZ, 1954, pp. 161–168; T. W. Manson, *Jesus and the Non-Jews*, 1955; G. F. Vicedom, *Missio Dei*, 1958; J. Hermelink, H. J. Margull, *Basileia* 1959, pp. 27–59; D. Bosch, *Die Heidenmission in der Zukunftschau Jesu* (Abhandlungen zur Theologie des Alten und Neuen Testaments 36), 1959, pp. 184–192; K. Barth, *Kirchliche Dogmatik*, IV, 3, pp. 337–353.

3. O. Michel, *Menschensohn und Völkerwelt*, p. 258.

4. I lack the opportunity to check as to whether the exegesis proposed by O. Michel is supported by other exegetes. The connection between Matt. 28: 16–20, and Dan. 7: 13–14, was of course recognized earlier, but without its consequences being drawn. So, for example, an observation in L. Goppelt, *Typos*, 1939, pp. 112–113: "The expressions by which the resurrected one speaks of his *exousia* (authority), Matt. 28: 18, depend upon Dan. 7: 14." The exegesis proposed by Michel is now almost universally recognized as correct. In the text we quote Michel's exposition of the connection with the Old Testament *in extenso*, but without the notes he adds. The original passage may be found in O. Michel, EMZ, 1941, pp. 261–262. The spacing is Michel's own.

5. E. Lohmeyer points this out, *op. cit.*, ad hoc.

6. Michel, *op. cit.*, p. 262, note 16.

7. Cf. Matt. 24: 14, Mark 13: 10. *Panta ta ethnē* is synonymous with *hē holē oikoumenē*, cf. O. Michel, TWNT V, pp. 159–161 "oikoumenē"; M. Paeslack, *Die Oikumene im Neuen Testament*, Theologia Viatorum (Berlin) II, 1950, pp. 33–47; D. Bosch, *op. cit.*, pp. 161–163.

J. C. Hoekendijk, *Kerk en Volk in de Duitse Zendingswetenschap*, 1948, p. 229, recalls how G. Warneck, M. Frick, and others "(have) heard (in the *panta ta ethnē*) an invitation to lose oneself in the ethnic structure of the object of mission". How little Matt. 28: 18–20 can be employed to find a Biblical foundation for "nation" or a "national mission" appears in TWNT II "ethnos" (G. Bertram and K. L. Schmidt), pp. 362–370.

R. K. Orchard, *Out of Every Nation* (I.M.C. Research Pamphlets, no. 7, S.C.M. Press, London 1959), poses the question as to the significance of the nations in the Bible. "For this is one of the points at which missionary action is held up or is in uncertainty for lack of theological clarification," p. 50. In continental European circles this question has been under discussion for a long time. As early as 1929, G. Bertram (in G. Rosen and G. Bertram, *Juden und Phönizier*, J. C. B. Mohr, Tübingen) emphasized the fact that the concept "people" (or "nation"—German *Volk*) in the Old Testament does not have a national but a religious significance; and in this way the significance of peoples/nations *or* (!) the heathen/Gentiles is also characterized. In the same direction we find G. von Rad, *Das Gottesvolk in Deuteronomium*, Kohlhammer, Stuttgart 1929, p. 19. The investigation of L. Rost, *Die Bezeichnungen für Land und Volk im Alten Testament, Die Vorstufen von Synagoge und Kirche*, 1938, points in the same direction.

W. Eichrodt deals in a noteworthy way with the concept "*Volkstum*" (nationality) in *Gottesvolk und die Völker*, where this eminent Old Testament scholar operates in certainly a very uncritical way, and in any event in a non-Biblical way, with a dialectical national concept, EMM, 1942. A good insight into this problem of Church and nation (*Volk*) is given by N. A. Dahl, *Das Volk Gottes*, 1941. We must further point out the significance of the Old Testament word *qāhal* (see TWNT "ekklesia") and the New Testament words *ethnos, laos*, and the like. For several years a Dutch-German study commission has been at work (on the initiative of the Deutsche Evangelische Missionsrat) on the problem of Church and nation (*Volk*). But the reports and discussion have never, alas, been published. With the permission of the writer I quote here the following statements from one of the reports: "Not what is suitable to a nation (*Volk*), but what is suitable to revelation, dominates." "The Old Testament preaches lastly a theocracy and not an ethnocracy" (A. Hulst, *Kirche und Volk im Alten Testament*, unpublished report). Further, J. C. Hoekendijk, *op. cit.*, pp. 229–235 and passim; J. Blauw, *Goden en Mensen*, pp. 5–18.

It seems out of the question to me that any other "clarification" can be given from the theological side to the problem raised by Orchard. Does it not solve itself when, in listening to the message of the gospel, one does not allow himself to be disturbed by the extraneous noises which come from the outside? The fierce struggle in the German theory of mission around the concept of *Volk* (nation/people), as Hoekendijk has sketched it, could be a beacon for every church threatened by nationalistic temptations. "Nationalism is always religious" (G. v. d. Leeuw, *Phaenomenologie*, p. 250, quoted by Hoekendijk, *op. cit.*, p. 275). This is naturally not to deny that the diversity of nations also has significance for the Kingdom of God. But to employ an historical, political, sociological, or perhaps even racist concept of "people" (*Volk*) is out of the question; in the light of the Bible the nations are to be viewed as signs (1) of God's will to peace (Gen. 10), (2) of His dominion over Israel (Deut. 32: 8, where the LXX even thinks of angels). God's activity with the nations as political powers has the purpose (1) of leading them to seek God (Acts 17: 26 f.), (2) of leading them to express the variegated wisdom of God in accepting the gospel (Eph. 3: 10) and to lift their voice in the many-voiced chorus that celebrates the praise of God (Rev. 7: 9). But we must note here that there is never any reference in the Bible to a congregation of a nation (*Volksgemeinde*) but only to a congregation from the nations. This has been rightly pointed out by K. Hartenstein and W. Freytag in a courageous witness at the time of a demonic over-excitement of nationalism in their land. The concepts of "people" (*Volk*) and "nation" are like so many other concepts which we accept as almost self-evident (such as culture, art, and the like): they take on no emphasis in the Bible except in their significance (whether favourable or unfavourable) for the salvation which God brings about. They belong to the area of the "powers" about which Paul speaks.

Theological discussion on this topic is coming more and more into prominence, since the passing of the first half of the century, in which the only interest in this concept, so important in Paul's thinking, was from a history-of-religion point of view. See, among others, O. Dehn, *Engel und Obrigkeit*, in *Theologische Aufsätze für K. Barth zum 50. Geburtstag*, Ch. Kaiser Verlag, Munich 1936, pp. 90–106, in which the "powers" are one-sidedly viewed as powers of the state; G. Kittel, *Christus und Imperator*, Kohlhammer, Stuttgart 1939 (opposed to Dehn's conception); O. Cullmann, *Königsherrschaft Christi und Kirche im Neuen Testament*, Zollikon Verlag, Zürich 1941; *Christus und die Zeit*, 1946, especially pp. 169–186; TWNT II "dynamis", pp. 286–328, and the literature there cited (W. Grundmann); *idem*, pp. 568–570 "exousia" (W. Foerster), etc. In the Netherlands, H. Berkhof has given an excellent introduction, though it is perhaps too concise, *Christus en de machten*, G. F. Callenbach, Nijkerk 1953, which would be well worth translating into English, given the reality of the problem.

8. For the concept "make disciples", cf. K. H. Rengstorf, TWNT IV, "manthanō," etc., pp. 417–464.

9. Here, it seems to me, we have a strong weapon against the methods employed in various fundamentalist (and other!) missions to make being a Christian dependent on the keeping of a series of commandments which, *apart* from the bond to Jesus Christ, must mean only a new enslavement to the powers of this world for those who would be made disciples of Jesus. At the same time I think we have here a contra-indication against those who conceive of the call to mission simply as a proclamation, and who want even to avoid any appearance of "conversion" or activity of conversion in missions!

10. This reference to the Sermon on the Mount is due to G. Eichholz in a meditation on Matt. 28: 18–20, in *Herr, tue meine Lippen auf*, pp. 282–294, E. Müller Verlag, Wuppertal Barmen 1957.

11. So Michel, *op. cit.*, p. 265.

12. *Ibid.*, p. 265.

13. Here, I think, lies the most pregnant justification for what is ordinarily called the "comprehensive approach". But at the same time the character and the boundaries of this comprehensive approach are shown in the personal form ("all that *I* have commanded you"): the approach must be carried by and must lead to a more distinct discipleship of the exalted Lord. Though personally I shrink a bit from burdening Scriptural data such as these too heavily with our present-day phrasing of questions (the danger of eisegesis is very great!), I still think that we may find here a directive for the present relationships between older and younger Churches. Can one, in the complicatedness of today's relationships, "teach them to observe all that I have commanded you" in every respect without the experience

of the whole Church in the whole world? Even if no "abridged gospel" were passed on by the "older" Churches to the "younger" ones, nevertheless, the evangelical *perspective* is often abridged as a consequence of a conception of "what is commanded" which is all too spiritualized. Here a deficiency from the past can be made up without the "older" Churches lapsing into a nineteenth-century method of pedagogy in missions.

14. The expressed promise of Christ's presence till the consummation of the world seems to be more an argument *against* than *for* the total or partial equalization of resurrection and Parousia, as in H. W. Bartsch, among others, in *Basileia* 1959, pp. 27–41, though he willingly grants that "mission belongs to the epiphany". But it is precisely the characteristic of the New Testament message that *in spite* of the eschatological character of Christ's resurrection (and thus of mission), it is not anticipated at the consummation or the Parousia. In the final conclusion of Bartsch's, "The Parousia has already happened and yet is awaited at the same time with every manifestation of His lordship" (p. 41), the problem is certainly put off, but not solved, because the word "Parousia" here has another meaning than "the Second Coming of the Lord" in the ordinary theological and (I think) Biblical significance.

15. We are reproducing here systematically what has also been expressed in the *Report regarding the Biblical foundations of Mission*, De Heerbaan, 1951, pp. 197–221, esp. pp. 207–208. See also W. Freytag, *Vom Geheimnis der Mission*, EMZ, 1940, pp. 97–98; *Mission im Blick aufs Ende*, EMZ, 1942, pp. 321–328; H. Schlier, *Die Entscheidung für die Heidenmission in der Urchristenheit*, EMZ, 1942, pp. 166–182, 208–212; M. A. C. Warren, *The Truth of Vision*, Canterbury Press, London 1948; Warren (ed.), *The Triumph of God*, a symposium, Longmans, London 1948; K. Hartenstein, *Mission und Eschatologie*, EMZ, 1950, pp. 33–42; H. N. Ridderbos, *De Komst van het Koninkrijk*, 1950, passim. For a survey of the development in international mission circles: H. J. Margull, *Theologie der missionarischen Verkündigung*, 1959, pp. 24–78 (with an excellent bibliography). In this context I thought it not necessary to deal with the discussion on the authenticity of Matt. 28: 18–20, since A. von Harnack, W. Bousset and others have written about this subject. See the commentaries. For me the manifold criticisms of this authenticity have never seemed convincing.

16. An extended discussion of the various types of "call to mission" which have here been pointed out concisely is beyond the compass of this survey. For the rest, I do not know of any comparative discussion of these *loci classici* up to now. Such a discussion, if one kept in mind the particular character of the gospels and thus the varieties of background, would contribute not a little to the clarification of our under-

standing of the "Biblical foundations and motives" of mission.

17. If we have emphasized the resurrection, the crowning of Christ's work as a condition for mission among the Gentiles, rather than the rejection of the Messiah by Israel, as has happened in most publications to date, then we wish now to express the fact that, as far as we can see, the rejection of Jesus Christ by Israel is not as much the condition for the mission to the Gentiles as the resurrection. By this rejection the path is also opened *to* the resurrection, via the cross. Furthermore, this rejection is partly revoked *after* the resurrection and the outpouring of the Holy Spirit (see the Acts of the Apostles). I think we must make a distinction between conditions for the mission to the Gentiles and the path along which this condition has come into being. Israel's rejection belongs to this path. I think we do an injustice to the shadings of the New Testament image when we view Israel's rejection of the Messiah *and* His resurrection as identical or similar conditions for the proclamation of the gospel among the nations.

I should like to resist with still greater emphasis the conclusion, drawn among others by H. Schlier, *Die Entscheidung für die Heidenmission in der Urchristenheit*, EMZ, 1942, p. 167, that by the rejection of the Messiah *Israel herself is rejected as the chosen people*. Further study of the New Testament on this subject has made me realize that my approval of H. Schlier at this point (in my *Goden en Mensen*, 1950, p. 115) was too rash and even incorrect. The problem of post-Christian Israel is, however, too comprehensive to be dealt with in any satisfactory way in this survey. I think it would be better to say that *after* the resurrection and outpouring of the Holy Spirit, the exclusive prerogatives of Israel as the people of God were (temporarily?) taken away and withheld. But this is no rejection; cf. Rom. 9–11. Another view is put forward by D. Bosch, *op. cit.*, in his (too) extreme conclusions, p. 92, that are incompatible with his remarks on p. 91: "Is the Messiah now to reject his people too? The Acts of the Apostles answers 'No'."

18. W. Michaelis, *Geist Gottes und Mission nach dem Neuen Testament*, EMM, 1932, pp. 5–16.

19. O. Michel, *Der Heilige Geist in der Völkerwelt*, EMZ, 1941, p. 327; K. Barth, *Kirchliche Dogmatik*, IV, 3, pp. 405–424.

20. H. Schlier, *op. cit.*, pp. 179–180.

21. Otherwise: R. Liechtenhan, *Die urchristliche Mission*, p. 50: "There exists no evidence that the primitive community offered any opposition on principle to the reception of Gentiles into membership. . . . It was only the concrete mission which the apostles did not welcome." This "concrete mission" still exists, I think, in the fact that the *resistance* had to be overcome.

22. This series has already been pointed out, particularly by O. Cullmann in *Christus und die Zeit*, part I, pp. 31–103, especially pp. 91–103.

23. Whether we are also to see in 2 Cor. 9 an evidence of the central position of the congregation at Jerusalem (*'ebhyônîm* as a designation of the congregation) seems to me too uncertain, still, in the present state of the discussion, for us to be able to pass judgment on it.

24. On the eschatological role of Jerusalem see D. Bosch, *Die Heidenmission in der Zukunftschau Jesu*, 1959, pp. 88–92, in which the most important literature is also cited. Since the publication of this survey there has appeared J. C. de Young's *Jerusalem in the New Testament. The significance of the city in the history of redemption and in eschatology* (Diss. Free University of Amsterdam), J. H. Kok, Kampen 1960.

To what extent Jerusalem will continue to play a role in the future is a question which cannot be answered here. See R. Martin-Achard, *Israel et les Nations*, p. 71: "Nevertheless it seems that, according to the witness of the New Testament, Jerusalem is still to play a role in the future. We would have to state in detail and examine how the assembling of mankind around Christ is to be harmonized with the eschatological function of the city of David." The study by Young, mentioned above, does not give an answer to this question.

25. R. Martin-Achard, *op. cit.*, p. 71.

26. *Ibid.*, p. 71: "The difference between the centripetal and centrifugal movements is only relative." Another motive is stated in a note: "If the mission of the New Testament seems at first glance centrifugal, it is to enable it to be centripetal. We go out into the world to gather it together; we cast the net to draw it in; we sow to reap." (J. J. von Allmen, by letter.)

The question of centripetal and centrifugal seems to be more important than it is represented here; see the text.

27. Note the nuance in comparison with Matt. 13: 19, where the seed is the *word* of the Kingdom. Are the children of the Kingdom, then, not the "word become flesh," as it were, of the Kingdom?

28. On this point see N. A. Dahl, *Das Volk Gottes*, especially part III, pp. 146–278. Further, G. von Rad, K. G. Kuhn, W. Gutbrod in TWNT III, "Israel", pp. 356–394; K. Emmerich, *Die Juden*, Zollikon Verlag, Zürich 1939; etc. etc. We have represented here the opinion of Dahl, *op. cit.*, pp. 213, 240, 243, 252, 253.

29. For this section see:

Joh. Warneck, *Paulus im Lichte der heutigen Heidenmission*, Berlin, 2nd ed. 1914.

R. Allen, *Missionary Methods: St. Paul's or ours*, London 1912, 4th ed. 1956.

A. Oepke, *Die Missionspredigt des Apostels Paulus*, Leipzig 1920.

R. Liechtenhan, *Der Apostel Paulus, sein Werk und seine Welt*, Basel 1928.

J. Richter, *Die Briefe des Apostels Paulus als missionarische Sendschreiben*, Gütersloh 1929.

K. Pieper, *Paulus*.

J. Holzner, *Paulus*, Herder & Co., Freiburg im Breisgau 1937.

R. Liechtenhan, *Die urchristliche Mission*, Zwingli Verlag, Zürich 1946.

G. F. Vicedom, *Die Rechtfertigung als gestaltende Kraft der Mission*, Freimund Verlag, Neuendettelsau 1952.

D. v. Swigchem, *Het missionair karakter van de christelijke gemeente volgens de brieven van Paulus en Petrus*, J. H. Kok, Kampen 1955.

30. R. Liechtenhan, *Die urchristliche Mission*, p. 78.

See also: Clarence Tucker Craig, *The Beginning of Christianity*, Abingdon-Cokesbury Press, New York Nashville 1943, p. 164: We should picture him (Paul) as one missionary among many, not yet the pioneering leader.

31. F. W. Grosheide, *De openbaring Gods in het Nieuwe Testament*, J. H. Kok, Kampen 1953, p. 136.

32. This expression was coined by N. A. Dahl during the European Consultation on The Word of God and the Church's Missionary Obedience, Geneva, July 11–14, 1960.

33. See Schneider, "ektrooma", TWNT II, pp. 463–465.

34. See R. Liechtenhan, *Die urchristliche Mission*, pp. 59–67.

35. *Ibid.*, pp. 77–84.

36. This refers to the *theological* impossibility of linking proselyte mission and Christian mission. This does not deny that *in practice* the missionary tradition of proselytism made its influence felt. The world of the gospel, however, is completely different from that of post-exile Judaism. Please see: E. Stauffer, *Jesus, Gestalt und Geschichte*, Dalp Taschenbücher 332, Francke Verlag, Berne & Munich 1960. (E.T. *Jesus and His Story*.)

37. For the "conversation with Israel," "the Christian approach to the Jews," I think it is important to attend to the double line of Paul's thinking. One cannot defend the priority of "the approach to the Jews" on the basis of Paul's declarations on the Gentile Christians as proselytes of Israel, because other passages can be placed alongside these which accentuate the quite special character of the Church over against Israel. But for the same reasons one cannot defend the priority of the mission to the Gentiles either. A theology which presses the idea of "Israel" too far is liable to fall into the same error as did the old Israel earlier: accentuating the *chosenness* instead of the act of divine choosing (election), which election was *for service*. The correct attitude is perhaps given in Rom. 15: 7–9. The whole problem of a

non-believing Israel must not take our attention here any further. It seems plain to me, on the basis of Rom. 9–11, that Paul saw his work among the Gentiles as the best and only way to continue to do something with his days for an Israel which was for the most part callous. See D. v. Swigchem, *Het missionair karakter van de christelijke gemeente volgens de brieven van Paulus en Petrus*. J. H. Kok, Kampen 1955, pp. 203–204.

38. It seems to me that this interdependence has never been given its due importance in the actual practice of Christian missionary work. We cannot discuss the many and various interpretations of the "fullness of Israel" and "all of Israel"; I would refer to the commentaries: quot commentationes tot sententiae!

39. O. Weber, *Kirchenmission? Eine Mission in gegliederter Vielfalt*, EMZ, 1960, pp. 129–140.

40. We refer for the question of the *Naherwartung* to E. Stauffer, *Jerusalem und Rom*, passim; Dalp Taschenbücher 331, Francke Verlag, Berne & Munich 1957.

41. R. Liechtenhan, *Die urchristliche Mission*, pp. 75–76.

Chapter 7

1. For this section in general see, among others, the works cited in notes 2 and 15 of chapter 6, and further, O. Cullmann, *Christus und die Zeit*, 1946; P. Althaus, *Die letzten Dinge*, 5th ed., 1949; G. Rosenkranz, *Weltmission und Weltende*, 1951; J. Munck, *Paulus und die Heilsgeschichte*, 1954; K. Barth, *Kirchliche Dogmatik*, IV, 3, 1959, pp. 337–424 and pp. 782–1034, and especially pp. 999–1007.

2. O. Michel, *Grundlagen des Denkens Jesu*, EMM, 1953, pp. 35–36.

3. The expression is from Jean Daniélou, *Essai sur le mystère de l'histoire*, 1954, p. 193.

4. W. Freytag, *Vom Sinn der Weltmission*, EMM. 1950, p. 74. If I see it correctly, this thought stands directly opposed to those which have been expressed by A. A. van Ruler, who lays a very great emphasis in his publication on the Christianization of the world. See, among others, his *Theologie des Apostolates*, EMZ, 1954, in which, for the rest, the various aspects which are offered there mitigate and define earlier publications in this area.

5. O. Cullmann, *Christus und die Zeit*, p. 138.

6. *Ibid.*, p. 141. See also O. Cullmann, *Eschatology and Mission in the New Testament*, in: W. Davies and D. Daube (ed.), *The Background of the New Testament and its Eschatology, Studies in Honour of C. H. Dodd*, Cambridge Univ. Press, 1956, pp. 409–422.

7. *Ibid.*, p. 140, pp. 145–146.

8. See also W. Freytag, *op. cit.*, p. 74; D. Bosch, *op. cit.*, pp. 165–169,

171. Bosch objects to calling mission a sign or portent, "because it is completely unpredictable". It seems to me a misunderstanding of the word "sign" to see in it any aspect of "predicting". I feel therefore that Bosch's objection is invalid, or at least *this* basis for his objection.

9. So W. Andersen, *Towards a Theology of Mission*, I.M.C. Research Pamphlet No. 2, S.C.M. Press, London 1955, pp. 36–40. See also: H. J. Margull, *Theologie der missionarischen Verkündigung*, 1959, pp. 24–38.

10. Stephen Neill's book, *Creative Tension*, 1959, is, if I have understood it rightly, an attempt to reconcile continental European and Anglo-Saxon thought in a positive dialectic which arouses a "creative tension". (Doubleday, New York.)

11. See, for example, how a prominent spokesman from (Eastern) Orthodoxy rejects missions on the ground of the divisions of the Church which cripple witness and make it impossible (in *Basileia* 1959: The Metropolitan James of Melita, *The Orthodox Concept of Mission and Missions*, pp. 76–80). To me, as a non-Orthodox reader, this argument gives the impression that here history, particularly Church history, though not undermining the normativeness and validity of the Biblical witness, nevertheless makes it to a great degree relative. Further, this article is an impressive illustration of how indissolubly "mission and unity" are intertwined.

12. K. Barth, *Kirchliche Dogmatik*, IV, 3, pp. 874–875. In the following pages Barth points out (pp. 875–878) the hiatus that characterized the patristic, scholastic, and then the Reformation and post-Reformation doctrines of the Church. I think Barth is the first, and up to now the only, systematic theologian who sees the existence and the task of the Christian to lie in witness. Of particular importance in this regard is §72.2, "Die Gemeinde für die Welt," pp. 872–910. I believe, then, that in this passage the remark of Bishop Stephen Neill is out of date, *Creative Tension*, p. 111: "As far as I know, no one has yet set to work to think out the theology of the Church in terms of that one thing for which it exists."

13. K. Barth, *op. cit.*, p. 878.

14. N. Goodall, *Missions under the Cross*, Edinburgh House Press, London 1953, p. 22. W. Andersen, *op. cit.*, p. 58, answers affirmatively the question put by Goodall: "In our judgment an affirmative answer must be given to this question. The work of all other activities and responsibilities of the Church must be judged by its relationship to the end. This work is in a twofold sense direction to the end—temporally to the time of the end, and geographically to the ends of the earth." By this statement he repeats what has been said constantly since the time of Hartenstein and others, but he overlooks the particular set of problems at which Goodall was aiming. The sentences here

quoted occur, further. at the end of the chapter which bears the title, "Problems left unsolved at Willingen and their solution through the new line of approach that Willingen has made possible". I think the solution that is presented here is far too easy and too apodictic, and furthermore Andersen's view will have to fall under the criticism, offered in the text, in regard to eschatology as a prerogative of a theological foundation of "foreign missions".

15. W. Freytag, *Vom Sinn der Weltmission*, EMM, 1950, p. 75. See also his: *Meaning and Purpose of the Christian Mission*, IRM, April 1950. pp. 189 ff. Further, for the general contents of this section, see: M. A. C. Warren, *The Truth of Vision*, Canterbury Press, London 1948; *The Christian Mission*, S.C.M. Press, London 1951, 3rd ed. 1953; *The Christian Imperative*, S.C.M. Press, London 1955.

16. Stephen C. Neill, *Creative Tension*, Doubleday, New York 1959, pp. 81 ff.

17. *Ibid.*, p. 82.

18. During a consultation of the Sub-committee on Theology of Mission of the Study Department WCC/IMC in London, October 22–23, 1957.

19. W. Andersen, *Towards a Theology of Mission*, S.C.M. Press, London 1955, 2nd ed. 1956, p. 58.

20. If I am not mistaken, the data of Biblical theology which have been offered here demonstrate what has been affirmed on other grounds by such men as Hans Dürr, *Die Reinigung der Missionsmotive*, EMZ, 1951, pp. 2–10; *Sendung, einige Fragen und Erwägungen*, EMM, 1954, pp. 146–152; J. C. Hoekendijk, *Mission heute*, 1954 Studentenbund für Mission; Stephen C. Neill, *Creative Tension*, p. 111.

21. A. A. van Ruler, *Theologie van het Apostolaat*, p. 46.

22. W. Freytag, *op. cit.*, p. 75.

23. "Report of the Advisory Commission on the Main Theme of the Second Assembly—Christ, the Hope of the World," p. 18, in *The Christian Hope and the Task of the Church*, Harper Bros., New York 1954.

24. M. A. C. Warren, *The Christian Imperative*, pp. 126, 127, 128.

25. A. A. van Ruler, *Theologie van het Apostolaat*, 1954, pp. 14, 15.

26. K. Barth, *Kirchliche Dogmatik*, IV, 3, 1959, p. 1002.

27. P. S. Minear, *Gratitude and Mission in the Epistle to the Romans*, in *Basileia*, 1959, p. 47.

28. Nevertheless it is not without significance that Minear, *op. cit.*, p. 42, announces that Freytag was critical of locating the motive for mission in thankfulness. This is connected, I think, with Freytag's special emphasis on the element of *expectation* in the eschatological foundation of mission.

29. The sharpest distinction between proclamation of the gospel

in the immediate environment of the Church and that in distant lands is made by van Ruler in his *Theologie van het Apostolaat*, e.g. p. 44: "The relation of God to paganism is an entirely different one from His relation to an apostate Christendom. Therefore one cannot, and one should not, reduce to a common denominator the two forms of the apostolate, say in Europe and in Asia. . . . There is more than a practical, technical difference here. It is a deeply spiritual difference, a difference of theological principle." I would like to make here only a few observations, to raise questions:

(a) To what extent can one still speak, in the vast majority of situations, of an apostate Christendom? Can one not have become so post-Christian that he is for all practical purposes pre-Christian (though certainly not yet anti-Christian)? Can one make the judgment of post-Christian only when it is clear that there has already been a confrontation with the gospel? And how many areas are there not, where the Church has lived in such an introverted fashion that, contrary to her deepest nature and calling, she has not made known the truth so that the Gospel is still hidden? (Cf. 2 Cor. 4: 2, 3.)

(b) To what extent is the "corpus christianum" (still) present as a *corpus*, a body, and to what extent is it Christian? On the answer to this question depends the decision, I think, as to whether one does accept a distinction in *principle* as well as in *practice* between "mission" and "foreign mission".

(c) What significance has history had in Europe and America as a "progressing *Heilsgeschichte*"? To what extent does this impose permanent obligations in regard to the other continents? Without falling into the error of the "white man's burden", can one speak of a permanent vocation to *service* to the world other than arising from the gospel that makes servants for Christ's sake *all* of us over the *whole* world?

30. See, e.g. H. J. Margull, *Theologie der missionarischen Verkündigung*, Evang. Verlag, Stuttgart 1959, which gives an excellent bibliography; W. Andersen, *Towards a Theology of Mission*, S.C.M. Press, London 1955; G. F. Vicedom, *Missio Dei*, Ch. Kaiser Verlag, Munich 1958.

31. The expression is from the Dutch theologian O. Noordmans.

32. The trinitarian foundation of mission is accepted generally and well known, too, I assume. See among others, Barth, *Auslegung von Matth. 28: 16–20*.

33. W. Freytag, *Vom Sinn der Weltmission*, EMM 1950, p. 75.

34. One thinks here of the tension between "Inter-church Aid" and Mission, behind which there is sometimes an attempt even to see a theological problem; and of the contrast which is often suggested between "missionary" and "pastoral", and the like. Over against

the inclination in the past to undervalue the theological character of missionary problems (Edinburgh 1910, Jerusalem 1928), it seems to me now that the inclination is strong to overvalue it, such as framing questions of administration as theological questions.

35. These words are taken from a recent pamphlet written by me: *De Weg der Zending*, J. H. Kok, Kampen 1960, p. 48.

36. This quotation I took from a leaflet of the Ch. Kaiser Verlag, Munich, who will publish before long selected writings of Professor Freytag.

37. For this passage see, among others, the following commentaries: H. L. Strack and P. Billerbeck, *Kommentar zum Neuen Testament aus Talmud und Midrasch*, Vol. IV, 1926; C. H. Beck, Munich, 2nd ed. 1956; H. Windisch, *Handbuch zum Neuen Testament, Die Katholischen Briefe*, J. C. B. Mohr, Tübingen 1930; E. G. Selwyn, *The First Epistle of St. Peter*, Macmillan, London 1947, 2nd ed. 1949; F. W. Beare, *The First Epistle of St. Peter*, Basil Blackwell, Oxford 1947, revised ed. 1958; A. Schlatter, *Erläuterungen zum Neuen Testament*, 9 Teil, Calwer Verlag, Stuttgart 1950; F. Hauck, *Das Neue Testament Deutsch*, 4 Band, Vandenhoeck & Rupprecht, Göttingen 1956; TWNT I "hagios" (O. Procksch), "aretē" (F. Büchsel), "basileia" (K. L. Schmidt), "genos" (F. Büchsel); III "hiereus" (G. Schrenk). Further: W. Bieder, *Grund und Kraft der Mission nach dem I Petrusbrief*, Zollikon Verlag, Zürich 1950, pp. 3–17; E. G. Selwyn, *Eschatology in 1 Peter*, in: W. Davies, D. Daube (ed.), *The Background of the New Testament and its Eschatology, Studies in honour of C. H. Dodd*, Cambridge Univ. Press, 1956, pp. 394–401.

38. E. G. Selwyn, *Eschatology in 1 Peter*, p. 394.

39. G. Schrenk, *op. cit.*, pp. 250–251.

40. Cf. what has been said about Exod. 19: 5–6 in Chapter 1.

41. Cf. Rom. 1: 21.

42. P. S. Minear has called attention to the proclamation among the Gentiles as *doxology*, and rightly so: *Gratitude and Mission in the Epistle to the Romans*, in *Basileia*, 1959, pp. 42–48.

ABBREVIATIONS

AMZ   Allgemeine Missions Zeitschrift
EMM   Evangelisches Missions Magazin
EMZ   Evangelische Missions Zeitschrift
IRM   International Review of Missions
NAMZ   Neue A—M—Z
TWNT   Theologisches Wörterbuch zum Neuen Testament, begun under G. Kittel
ZAW   Zeitschrift für die alttestamentliche Wissenschaft

GENERAL BIBLIOGRAPHY

H. H. Rowley (ed.), *Eleven Years of Bible Bibliography* 1946–1956, The Falcon's Wing Press, Indian Hills, Colorado, U.S.A., 1957

G. H. Anderson, *Bibliography of the Theology of Missions in the 20th Century*, Missionary Research Library, New York, 1958

Raymond P. Morris, *A Theological Book List*, produced by The Theological Education Fund of the International Missionary Council, 1960, and distributed by Blackwell's, Oxford, England, and Allenson's, Napierville, Illinois, U.S.A.

INDEX OF BIBLE REFERENCES

M

178

INDEX OF AUTHORS

Printed in the United Kingdom
by Lightning Source UK Ltd.
120147UK00001B/51